In Grandmother Gell's Kitchen

A selection of recipes used
in the Eighteenth Century

Carol Barstow

Biography

Carol is Librarian at Bromley House Library in Nottingham, an independent subscription library situated in a former Georgian town house in the city centre. Her love of history and of cooking combined in 1994 when she undertook the MA in Local and Regional History at the University of Nottingham, writing her dissertation on 'Kitchens and Cooking from 1650-1800'. In order to practice this sort of cooking in an authentic setting (and wearing period clothing) Carol has spent several summers cooking with the Sealed Knot, and takes part in living history weeks for schools at Bullace Hill near Chepstow. At home she cooks for comparatively fewer: living in a cottage in North Nottinghamshire with two adult children and a dog. Three hens supply the family with all the eggs they need.

Acknowledgements

My first thanks has to be to the staff at Nottinghamshire Archives, always friendly and helpful whilst I was transcribing the manuscripts, and never seeming to mind my being last out on a Tuesday evening. Mark Dorrington has been an encouraging and patient editor.

My mother taught me to love cookery, especially baking and making jam, so without her this book would never have happened. My family and friends have tasted and commented, usually positively, on many of these recipes. Bromley House members have helped to eat the produce of my weekend baking sessions, and listened to me as I enthused about the cooking methods. Many others have humoured me during this project, my daughter Beth joined me at Sealed Knot events and my son Chris has waited for me to bake 'proper cakes' again.

Copyright

Front Cover : Great Kitchen, Sulgrave Manor (Photograph: Charles Glenn)

Back Cover : Drawing of Hopton Hall from the Eighteenth Century (DRO D3258/8/53)

ISBN: 978-0-902751-63-7

Printed and designed by: Nottinghamshire County Council, Design, Publications and Print 2009

In Grandmother Gell's Kitchen

1. Front and back cover of first book (NA DD/E/59/56)

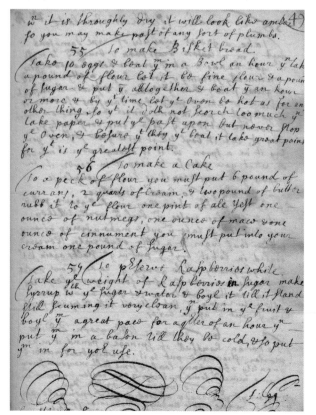

w^n it is throughly dry it will look like amber
so you may make past of any sort of plumbs.

55   To make Bisket bread.

Take 10 eggs & beat y^m in a Bowl an hour y^n take
a pound of flour let it be fine flour & a pound
of sugar & put y altogether & beat y an hour
or more & by y^t time let ye oven be hot as for an
other thing so y^t it doth not scorch too much y^n
take paper & put ye past upon but never stop
ye oven, & besure y^t they y^t beat it take great pains
for y^t is ye greatest point.

56   To make a Cake

To a peck of flour you must put 6 pound of
currans, 2 quarts of cream & two pound of butter
rubb it to ye flour one pint of ale Yest one
ounce of nutmegs, one ounce of mace & one
ounce of cinnamon you must put into your
cream one pound of sugar

59   To pserve Raspberries white

Take ye weight of Raspberries in sugar make a
syrrup wth y^e sugar & water & boyl it till it stand
still scuming it very clean, y^n put in y^e fruit &
boyl y^m a great pace for a qtter of an hour y^n
put y^m in a bason till they be cold, & so put
y^m in for yor use.

2. Recipes from page 49 of third book (NA DD/E/59/58)   3. Front cover of recipes copied by Thomas Gell (NA DD/E/59/58)

1. Introduction

This book originated in the research for my dissertation for the MA in Local and Regional History at the University of Nottingham, when the topic I looked at was 'Kitchens and Cooking from 1650 – 1800'. One of the pleasures of the research was reading and trying various recipes from this period. One collection which intrigued me was that described as 'The receipt book of Grandmother Gell', held at Nottinghamshire Archives with the documents deposited by the Edge family of Strelley Hall. It was to this collection that I returned, to transcribe the complete collection, and to provide workable modern versions for those like myself who have a fascination with food from the past. It is a selection of these recipes that are published here.

1.1 The Manuscripts

The recipe collection is in three parts, and several different hands. The first[1] is written into a home made book, and appears to be in three hands. The main hand writes on the right hand page of the book, which was later continued in a different hand by a second person who was writing in 1750, as there is a dated recipe for raisin wine. The left page is written in a less literate hand and these recipes are marked with an S. There are 97 recipes altogether plus one on a loose sheet of paper. Many are attributed to someone, i.e. 'Mrs Clay's way to...'

The second home made book[2] is inscribed 'Thomas Gell', and is clearly a copying out of recipes from three different books, as he marks in Latin where he has finished each book. The recipes are numbered, and an index has been compiled. The handwriting is neat and consistent. There are 239 recipes, the grouping and wording would suggest that one section has been copied from a published cookery book, and there are references to Hartman's 'Family Physitian'[3]. There is a separate section on perfumes of various kinds. There is also a sheet with menu plans for three meals, with places and dates given. The book gives the impression of much use, being rather worn and having food stains.

The third collection[4] is written on pages from an accounts book, in different handwriting to the other collections. Some loose sheets are included with recipes written on the back of letters or scraps of paper. Some of these have been copied into the accounts pages, so are duplicates. One recipe is dated May ye 2nd 1750. There are 263 recipes in these pages.

Each manuscript contains a mixture of recipes for foods and drinks, with medicinal recipes, including some for horses. There are no exact repetitions from one collection to another, although you can tell family favourites from different versions of the same recipe, and some have been annotated with 'This is good'. There is a bias in the collection towards cakes and biscuits, something I have complete sympathy with.

---

1. Nottinghamshire Archives DDE 59/56
2. Nottinghamshire Archives DDE 59/58
3. Hartman, George *'The Family Physitian...'*, London, 1696
4. Nottinghamshire Archives DDE 59/57

1.2 The Gells and Hopton Hall

The Gell family and their heirs were resident in the Wirksworth area of Derbyshire from at least 1327[5], until 1986. Hopton Hall was built in the late sixteenth century by a Thomas Gell, on a H shaped plan. In 1670, when the Hearth Tax was calculated, the Hall had 13 hearths liable for tax, giving the impression of a comfortable, if not grand, home. Plans suggest that an earlier house with a great hall may have been incorporated into the building. After the death of Thomas, his widow married Sir John Curzon of Kedleston, and her sons went to live with her there. The eldest son of Thomas, Sir John Gell (1593-1671), married Elizabeth Willoughby of Wollaton Hall, Nottingham. Sir John played a prominent role in in the Parliamentarian cause in the 1640s, but was later suspected of plotting against the Commonwealth. He was imprisoned and his estates were confiscated, being returned by Charles II in 1660.

Sir Philip Gell (1651-1719), grandson of Sir John I, succeeded to the estate after his father died without children. In a very complicated will, he left the estate to his unmarried sister Temperance for the rest of her life, and then to his 'wellbeloved' nephew John Eyre, son of his sister Catherine. There were several conditions to the inheritance, John was to change his name to Gell, take the Coat of arms of Gell, and must reside at Hopton Hall. He fulfilled these conditions to inherit Hopton Hall in 1730. Sir Philip in a codicil of his will, requested Thomas Gell, of Wirksworth, Chirurgen (Surgeon) to be one of the Trustees for Almshouses that he was building in the town of Wirksworth. It seems certainly possible and even likely that this Thomas, closely connected to the main family by friendship and also by blood (third cousin once removed to Sir Philip), is the one who copied out the recipes. If they were his Grandmother's, then they belonged to Cicily who married Anthony Gell in Wirksworth in 1648.

There is a plan of Hopton Hall[6] drawn in the eighteenth century but undated, inscribed with the names William and Katherine Eyre, John's parents. This lists the following rooms: It gives a snapshot of what the house was like around the time that John Eyre inherited it:

ye great parlor
a pasage to ye garden
ye great stair foot
ye halfepace of ye great stairs
ye drawing room
ye hall
ye taras walke [terrace walk]
a pasage
ye litle parlor

ye butery
ye seler stairs
ye passage to ye Kitch
ye kitchin
ye back stair foot
ye door in to ye back court
a pasage & stairs to ye larder
ye pastery

---

5. Maxwell Craven and Michael Stanley *'The Derbyshire Country House'*, Ashbourne, Derbyshire, 2004
6. Derbyshire Record Office D258/11/23

This drawing is of the main part of the house, and doesn't include any outbuildings. John Eyre Gell lived at Hopton until his death in 1739. An inventory[7] is taken of Hopton Hall in 1738/9 and lists in detail the contents of the house. In the inventory the following rooms are listed:

Kitchen	*Closett*
Kitchen closet	*Smoak Closett*
Upper Deary	*Inner Nursery*
Washhouse	*Passage by the red room*
Landry	*Other nursery*
Inner Deary	*Closett*
Old Parlour	*In the Linnen Press*
Old Hall	*Press in the passage*
Passage between Hall and Kitchen	*Maids room*
Pastery	*In the Lobbey*
Steward's room	*Little room near the lobby*
Little Pantry	*Purple room*
Servant's Hall	*Red room or best room*
Coal hole	*Garratt*
The passage to Brewhouse	*In the Mews Garratts*
The New Hall	*Middle Garratt*
Parlour	*Further Garratt*
Drawing Room	*Callico Room*
Dining Room upstairs	*Mr Buxford room*
White Chamber	*Blue Room*
Desert Room	*Long Gallery*
Library	*Parsons Room*
Red room over hall	*Green Room*
In the Closet	
Dressing room	

4. Inventory of John Eyre Gell 1738 (DRO D3287/8/53)

The contents of kitchen and other service rooms are given in detail and are as follows:

Kitchen

Land iron & froggs; two racks with hooks; four iron peggs and iron to place dishes on before the fire, Lazy back; two toasting forks. Three coal rakes; two beef forks; two gibbets; six pott hooks; two Pig plates; one grid Iron; two Irons to place over stove harths; a Chafeing dish & fire pan; an Iron stool; three iron clevers; a chopping knife; a smoak jack; two iron chains, a plate from a pair of wafer Irons; two iron Dripping pans; five frying pans; an iron ladle; twenty pair of tongs eighteen fire shovells; five iron pokers; six large spitts & one bird spit; an Iron Grate, seven Iron fenders; & one brass fender, a box Iron; five cutting knives; thirteen brass candlesticks; two pair of high snuffers; one snuffer case; two extinguishers; nine Sauce pans; four stew pans; five brass pans; four fish pans; two leaden fish plates & a tin one; a copper cesterne & a tin one; four skellets; three skimmers three brass Lamps; two basteing ladles; two tin Droppers; four brass potts; nine brass kettles; a brass lid; two candle boxes; two tin dish covers; a brass cullinder; four wood pott lids; a tin cake rim; a grater; an old iron pott; a brass pott with feet; five tea kettles; three brass Morters; three iron pestells; one brass pestell; a brass Boyler and wooden cover; a wooden salt box; a bacon natch; sixteen shelves; a brass rack over the sink; a Landsettle with a tin back; a forme; two chopping blocks, pair of bellows; three racks whereon the Guns lye; an Egg Slice; & an Iron to draw fowls; a tea Kitchen of copper; two brass pair of scales;two pair of wooden scales, a salamander or Devell, a plate baskett; two Pye boards; an iron oven mouth or door; five pewter rings; a salver; two cheese plates with feet; six mazarenes; two long Pye plates; Eight long pye plates; one large Dish for a chine of beef; fifty eight

Dishes; three pewter Measures; twenty three soop plates; Eleaven Dozen & seven table plates; two pewter Basons; a pewter Salt, a flower ark; ten trenshers; four wooded bowls; a back Sprittle; a beef Tub; a wooden Skreen; two tubs to wash Dishes; A Mung[8] barrell; five Lacon Sieves; two hair ones; three Rowling pins; two rasps for bread; a kneading Tub; with two Leather Baggs; a balance Snier with lead; a Mustard ball; seven brass petty pans and seventeen tin ones and a wooden chair; the ash pitt; grate; an iron Candlestick fixt in the kitchen window.

Kitchen closett

A Jelly Stand; a marble mortar and wooden pestell; a Land Iron; two little setts of Drawers; a chocolate pott and Mill; two tables; three chairs; a Buffett; a Coffee Mill.

Upper Deary

Four leaden Milk cesternes; large one and five lesser ones; twelve cheese fatts; four churns; two spreading rakes; two still bottoms; a form; a dresser; four shelves; a cheese press; a burned iron.

Inner Deary

A dresser on three sides

Pastery

Greet Mill

Little Pantry

A Napkin Press

In the Brewhouse

A Large Copper; a Leaden cooler; one mash fatt; a Large Gathering Tub; two Ladeing piggins; one tin Dish; one peal; and a Scope[9]; A wooden spout to convey liquour into the cooler; a wheel chair[10].

Plate

Three basons; one Moutaph; Nine Salvers; five tankards; seven candlesticks; a pair of snuffers & Dish; a sauce pan; two porringers; two coffee potts; two milk potts; Eight Tumblers; Six Castors; Six Salts; a tea kettle & a Lamp; a Tea Pott; a Square waiter; Eight forks; two ladles; a Marrow Spoon; four Dozen of Spoons; two Dozen of tea spoons; one childs spoon; Eleaven salt spoons; three pair of tea tongs; two sieve spoons; a colender Ladle.

A Shagareen[11] case with twelve silver hafted knives & the like number of silver hafted forks & twelve silver spoons.

A dozen of Silver Forks; two dozen more of large silver hafted knives; a Dozen of Lesser silver hafted knives & the like numbers of silver hafted forks; a gold Headed cane and a blood stone cane; a Jugg, a skimmer; two Dozen of Ivory hafted knives and two Dozen of Ivory hafted forks new ones.

Ten more Ivory Hafted knives & ten forks

Five old ivory hafted & as many forks.

---

8. Mung – variation of Mong, a mixture of different kinds of meal
9. Probably a scoop
10. A chair with a wheel back.
11. Untanned leather, usually coloured green.

The branch of the Gell family resident in Wirksworth lived at the Gate House which had been bought by Thomas Gell in the early eighteenth century. Of seventeenth century origins, the house was taxed at six hearths in 1670, a comfortable, though modest dwelling. At the Manor House in Wirksworth lived a branch of the Hurt family whose main seat was at Alderwasley. The Gell and Hurt families were linked by both marriage and friendship, and the Hurt families were also linked by marriage to the Edge family of Strelley. In 1785 Thomas Edge of Strelley married Elizabeth Hurt, and another Temperance Gell, either the niece of Sir Philip Gell or the daughter of Thomas Gell of the Gate House was one of the witnesses to the marriage. This may be the link through which these cookery books came to be among the Edge family records in Nottinghamshire Archives, and not with the rest of the Gell documents in the Derbyshire Record Office.

There are recipes attributed to various people in the collection, one section copied out by Thomas is marked 'Mrs Billings and Mrs Gallimore'. There are parish register entries for both these names in Wirksworth throughout the seventeenth and eighteenth century and in 1756 a Philip Gell is witness at a wedding for Thomas Gallemore.

There are several thousand items in the collection of Gell family papers in Derbyshire Record Office. There are recipes amongst those as well, some are medicinal, for horses as well as people, and others are culinary. The culinary recipes appear to be either 16th century or 19th century. There is also a tantalising reference in an 18th century letter about the 'receipt books having come to hand'.

1.3 Dating the recipes

Recipe collections are difficult to date, Thomas Gell copied three recipe books into one at around 1740. If they were his Grandmother's recipes then they may have been in use half a century earlier. Recipes have a long life, being passed from one generation to another, and contemporary cookery books went through many editions over a long period of time. A few of the recipes can be traced to published recipe books, all of which were published before 1695 but were still in print many years later. The style and ingredients used would suggest that these recipes originate from the later 17th century. What we can say for certain is that they were in use and valued in the mid eighteenth century.

1.4 Interpreting the recipes for today

The principal methods of cooking during this period were roasting and boiling on an open fire, whilst things that required a more gentle heat could have been cooked on a chaffing dish. Ovens for baking were brick built, either situated in a bakehouse, or next to the kitchen fire, and were heated by lighting a fire inside the oven. When this was swept out, the bricks retained enough heat to cook the food, starting with bread, then biscuits and cakes as the oven cooled, ending with tasks such as drying herbs. As the oven would be too hot to get close to, a wooden peel was used to put items in and take them out of the oven. Taking several hours to reach the correct temperature, baking days would have started early and finished late. Cooking temperatures, where given, are necessarily vague.

Measurements, too, are often vague. Spoon sizes would have varied, and eggs were smaller than ours are today. Pint sizes and weights could vary with the substance being weighed and measured.

Whilst many ingredients are familiar ones to us, others would have differed. Today for bread baking we use a hard imported wheat whereas a softer flour, more like our plain flour, would commonly have been used. White flour was available. It would have been bolted through a linen cloth and it would have been this flour which was generally used for cakes and biscuits, even if the general household bread was wholemeal or a mixture of wheat and rye. As there was no self raising flour or baking powder the only option for making cakes light was either yeast or well beaten egg. Yeast was used to raise many mixtures, or they have instructions such as *'beat for two hours'*. Many of the pies were designed to be self supporting, although pottery dishes or tin pie plates were available. Pottery dishes came into more common use towards the end of the eighteenth century when wheat was scarce, even for those not in straitened circumstances. To bake a free standing pie required a tough pastry case, capable of being put into the oven on the peel. In some cases the pastry was not necessarily eaten, though it could have been used to thicken soups and stews. This does not mean that food would have been wasted, what was not eaten by people would have been fed to pigs.

With an understanding of health relying on maintaining a warm and moist balance of the 'humours', foods were understood to have different properties of cold or warm, dry or wet. This led to recipes that would seek to counteract, or balance, the effects of different foods. For example, raw fruit was considered to be cold, but this could be rectified by cooking it with wine and spice. There is a tendency to use varying quantities of egg whites and yolks in recipes as whites were considered to be very damp and cold. Egg whites were also used to clarify various boiling liquids, making it easy to lift the scum off, so the spare whites would not have gone to waste.

All of the recipes that have been given a modern version have been tested. The selection reflects the original collection, although the cures and domestic recipes have been added for interest only. The other main omission is that of a modern version for wines and related drinks, interesting though they are, few people make wine at home today, so they are given as examples only. There is a bias towards recipes that will still appeal to the modern cook. They have been put into sections for ease of use, rather than left in the order in which they appear in the manuscripts. The sections reflect those found in contemporary cookery books of that period. Each section starts with recipes with a modern version. Then there is a selection of recipes which were common at the time, unlikely to be cooked today, but fascinating for the insights they give us into the food of our forebears. I have occasionally added a different title to make them more accessible, and suggestions as to how they could be served as part of a modern meal.

2. Meals in the Early Eighteenth Century

The recipes contained in the Gell manuscripts cover an unknown period of time, but we do know that they were in use or certainly of interest between 1728 and 1754 as these are dates recorded. From the nature of the recipes it is likely that they are older than this, although one has to allow for regional variation, particularly between London, the focus of society, and country regions, which may have lagged behind the current fashion. What follows here is a description of the eating patterns of the first half of the eighteenth century to put these recipes into context. This was in many ways a time of transition in eating habits when new ways of eating which were brought in from abroad with the Restoration became established in this country.

2.1 From Breakfast through to Supper

Breakfast, the first meal of the day, was taken when people rose, and at the beginning of the century, or out in the country, for working people, this would have been around 6 or 7am. A seventeenth century breakfast would have been beer or ale to drink, bread, cold meat, cheese, fish, with possibly a rich broth for something warm. In areas where they were grown, then an oatmeal pudding, either savoury or sweet, may have been eaten. Those with more leisure would have eaten later.

One major change altered this meal during this period. The hot drinks: tea, coffee and chocolate, had become popular. These drinks had been introduced in the late seventeenth century, and were now becoming established. Chocolate was always the most expensive of these, and was drunk mainly by those who would describe themselves as gentlemen, the Gell family certainly being in this class. Coffee and tea were drunk more widely than chocolate, although it would be some time before tea gained its universal popularity.

In this period, breakfast became more sophisticated for the more affluent and was served later, between 9am and 10am. Wiggs are a rich bread cake, most often flavoured with caraway seeds, and were very popular in the eighteenth century. They could be eaten with ale as a snack, and were certainly enjoyed for breakfast. They could be dunked if you liked, and perhaps if they had been kept for a while this might be a good idea. The Gells had eight different recipes for Wiggs so we can infer that these were a family favourite.

Thomas Gell also has a recipe for breakfast cakes – a rich baked breadcake similar in some ways to a muffin, but rolled out and cut, and baked in the oven. Spiced bread and various small cakes could also be served. Toast – described by Carl-Philip Moritz, visiting London in 1782, as *'necessary because the houses were so cold and the butter was so hard that it was only on toast that it was spreadable'*[12] found its continuing role on the breakfast table during this period.

12. Kate Colquhuon *Taste*, London 2007

One cannot think of toast without thinking of marmalade. There are numerous recipes for 'Marmalett', from this time, but this was not initially the breakfast spread we think of today. Marmalades originally had a place in the dessert course but during this period they were becoming part of the breakfast menu. They were a preserve, fruit having a short season needed to be kept, and there were various ways of doing this. A fruit paste, often stiff enough to cut with a knife, was one way to do this. Quince was the favoured fruit for Marmalatt, but orange was also popular.

Dinner was initially a midday meal and the main meal of the day, and if eaten then would have been followed by a supper between 5pm and 8pm.

As breakfast became later, so did dinner, and to fill the gap between the two a light luncheon would be served, which could be an informal snack. It seems likely that the Gells ordinarily had their dinner at midday, this can be surmised from instruction given about when to take a medicinal drink which features in the recipe collection.

Dinner, whenever it was served, was a substantial meal for those who could afford it. If guests were invited, the elaborate meal could last four or five hours. For a formal meal two courses were served, followed by a banquet, the word having a different meaning to how we use it today, being the dessert course. You would not be expected to eat from every dish.

The two main courses were a mixture of sweet and savoury. Arrangement was important, so much so that published recipe books would have elaborate fold out plans showing how to place dishes, and recipe books would comment that 'this is a good corner dish', apart from Hannah Glasse[13], who considered this an impertinence to instruct the housewife thus, on the part of the writer. Some dishes would be 'removes', to be taken off and replaced by others.

As for table settings and table manners - pewter was the favoured material although china was becoming more popular among the wealthy. Dinner was mainly eaten with a knife and spoon. Whilst forks had been used for serving messy things, such as fruits in syrup, they were slow to come into general personal use at the table. Indeed, it was quite a while before any provision of cutlery for guests would have been made. In the seventeenth century people would have carried their own knife and spoon with them. In 1669 a traveller to England commented on the lack of forks in the country[14]. When they did come into use, they were placed face downwards on the table, so as not to get caught on the frills of the cuffs. Finger bowls were placed on the table, although as forks came into fashion these went out. Napkins were not considered essential. Why use one if the tablecloth is large enough to be used for that purpose, including tucking into one's collar, and wiping one's mouth?

13. Hannah Glasse *The Art of Cookery made plain and easy,* Fascimile of the first edition, Prospect Books, 1995
14. Sara Paston-Williams *The art of dining,* National Trust Enterprises, 1993

Men and women would have been seated at each end of the table at formal occasions. We have mention of 'a new and promiscuous mode of seating' in 1788, when men and women were alternated. Etiquette stated that it was important not to eat too quickly or too slowly, the former showed you were too hungry, the latter that you didn't like the food. It was vulgar to eat your soup with your nose in your plate, and *It is exceeding rude to scratch any part of your body, to spit, to blow your nose…, to lean your elbows on the table, to sit too far from it, to pick your teeth before the dishes are removed'.*

The next course was the dessert - or banquet. This could have been served in a separate room, and may be the 'desert room' in the plan of Hopton Hall. If it was served at the same table, then at this point the cloths would be removed, and the polished wood of the dining table would form the backdrop for dishes meant to please the eye as well as the palate. It was time for the mistress of the house to show off her skills, although banquetting stuff could have been purchased from the confectioner.

This is when the elaborate 'marchpane' confections, from which our marzipan is derived, would have been produced. These were made in fancy shapes of varying sorts. Jellies were made by boiling calves feet or using hartshorn and were flavoured with fruit and wine. Preserved fruits in syrup, cream concoctions, delicate biscuits and wafers, and the marmaletts would be served as part of this banquet.

After the dessert and wine, it was time for the ladies to withdraw and drink tea and coffee elsewhere. At this point the men would turn their attention to some serious drinking with the drink of preference being port. Claret was considered a drink for boys, not men. A chamber pot would be kept in the room or provided nearby, as it was at Kedleston Hall, Derbyshire, so the flow of conversation would not be interrupted by a call of nature[15]. The men would join the ladies later for a restorative coffee.

There would have been a difference between what the affluent and those merely comfortably off ate. I think it is fair to assume that except when entertaining or celebrating a special event, one course with a variety of dishes would have been eaten by most households.

Although during the Commonwealth period following the Civil War fish days were abolished as being too popish, they were re-installed with the Restoration and are enshrined in the Book of Common Prayer. So, in theory at least, from 1660 onwards, the 40 days of Lent, the Ember Days, Rogation Days, days before certain feast days (16 in all), and all Fridays were to be kept as fast days. A fast day was one on which no meat products were eaten, rather than a complete fast. There were also a corresponding number of feast days. This would have a considerable impact on patterns of eating if they were kept strictly. There are several recipes described as Lenten recipes within the collections. A good example is Pottage Mager. As jellies were made using gelatine derived from calves' feet, there are recipes using gelatine derived from fish skin as an alternative.

15. Sara Paston-Williams *The art of dining*, National Trust Enterprises, 1993

There are many recipes for wine in the collection – raisin, cherry (both red and black) elder, orange, English grape, currant, gooseberry, sage, birch, artificial champagne, cyder royal, as well as mead. Perhaps these were served at family meals rather than port or claret.

If you have had a substantial dinner lasting four to five hours you would still, as a guest, be offered supper. You might be relieved to know this was a much lighter meal, usually just one course, although possibly it could be extended by a banquet. At its simplest it would be cold meat and bread. A warm drink would be served at this time – a posset – a rich warm spiced alcoholic beverage. The early versions of hot chocolate closely resembled the possets. The basic recipe was a mix of wine and cream, thickened with egg yolks, and sweetened and spiced.

5. Menu plans (NA DD/E/59/57/23)

2.2 The Menu Plans

Published recipe books included a diagram of a menu plan showing not only what dishes were served but where they were to be placed on the table. That menus have been written out and kept suggests that these occasions were special. They appear to have been written out retrospectively as they are not in chronological order, and given the varying venues are probably meals that the writer was a guest at rather than the cook. The precise dates given for two of these suggest they were part of the Christmas/New year celebration. They may have been copied from somewhere else but are on a loose sheet of paper in DDE 59/57 with the other loose sheets, with recipes also written on the same piece of paper. Whilst we are unable to know precisely who the hosts and guests were they show what a gentry family would have served as a meal when they had guests, and as such give us a much more valid indicator of such meals than a published cookery book. The grand idealised meal plans in those would be something to aspire to rather than actually enjoy for the majority of well to do families. The layout of the menu reflects the plans for meals that are found in the published cookery books, and shows that the positioning of the dishes was considered to be important in practice as well as theory.

Taking them chronologically that for 1728 comprises two courses, the first is all savoury, apart from the Mince pyes, the second a mixture of savoury and sweet. The first comprises 'made' dishes, the second two roasts, turkey and a haunch of venison. Turkey had come into England from the New World, and these were certainly available in London markets from the mid sixteenth century onwards. Burrs are sweetbreads (testicles), a delicacy of the time. Brawn is a dish made from a pig's head and trotters. Sillybubs are a frothy wine and cream concoction, hard work for someone as they need long periods of whisking. Scotch collops is a veal and egg dish – at its simplest this would be similar to our current bacon and eggs. There are recipes for these, and the Apple pudding in the collection. Most dishes are served on a base of bread. *'Lay it upon Sippets and so send it in'* is often the serving instruction.

At Dr Gell's 1728 Derby

	Fish	
Scotch Collops	*Mincd pyes*	*Stewed Hare*
	Venison pasty	

	A Turkey
Bak: pears	*App Pudding*
	Sillybubs
Burrs	*Lobster*
	H: Venison

The dinner at Hopton in 1752 would appear to be the most sophisticated of the three menus given, although it may simply be that we have more information on this meal. The pattern is similar here, with a savoury first course, mixed second course, then dessert. The dessert is an excellent example of the use of dried or preserved sweetmeats, cherries would certainly have been preserved in some form and it is likely that the apples were too. There are several recipes for lemon creams in the collection, these are rich but delicious. It is interesting that raisins were considered a part of the dessert course in their own right, rather than as an ingredient in other dishes.

Hopton Decemb^r 30th 1752

Soop		Ducks		Desert
Saltfish		Potted woodcock		Brandy'd Peaches
Avery large Coller of Brawn		Pudding		Pestachia Nutts Raisins
Rowld Mutton		Coller'd eel		Custard. Sillybubs Limon Cream
Haunch Venison		Minc'd Pyes		Dry'd Sweetmeats Almonds Apples Cherries

Red port, Claret, Champain, White Wine

Alderwasley in 1754 was the home of Charles and Catherine Hurt, and in 1751 their son Francis had married Mary Gell, daughter of Thomas Gell of the Gate House, Wirksworth. Again this menu features the favourites of a Haunch of Venison, prized as a roast, partly because of its royal connections, and Turkey. The Hurt estate included a deer park. Venison was often given as a gift in this period. It is a fairly simple menu, and does not include a desert course although that does not mean that one was not served.

Alderwasley Ja^ny 3^d 1754

Salmon			Sco'tch Collops		
Sauce	Sauce		Sillybubs	Minc'd Pyes	Sillybubs
Tongue	Pudding			Turkey	
Sauce	Sauce				
H Venison					

3. The Eighteenth Century Housewife

The role of the eighteenth century housewife was varied, and by no means restricted to the house. At a time when the terms 'husbandman' and 'husbandry' were used to express the role of the man around the farm and home, there was no sense that the woman's role was any less important than the man's. The classic contemporary book on the subject was that of Gervase Markham, first published in 1615, 'The English Housewife' and in print until 1683, so contemporary with these recipes. He had previously written about good husbandry. As well as being generally virtuous, clean and needing an endless amount of energy the role of the housewife was divided into several areas. A housewife's personal qualities should include virtue and religion, temperance, and she should dress in a way that promotes health rather than adheres to fashion, and is suitably modest. It is worth quoting Gervase Markham's conclusion on her personal qualities in full.

'To conclude, our English housewife must be of chaste thought, stout courage, patient, untired, watchful, diligent, witty, pleasant, constant in friendship, full of good neighbourhood, wise in discourse, but not frequent therein, sharp and quick of speech, but not bitter or talkative, secret in her affairs, comfortable in her counsels, and generally skilful in all the worthy knowledges which do belong to her vocation; of all or most parts whereof I now in the ensuing discourse intend to speak more largely.[16]

Whilst we may think of cookery as the most important part of the role of the housewife this is not the first one listed by Markham. Physical Surgery is the first section of his book, with a collection of remedies for various complaints. Many are made from herbs that are still used for the same complaints today, but even if they were proven to work there are many that we may not wish to try. What is evident from the recipes is that as well as familiarity with herbs and other medicines, the woman also needs skill in distilling, as many of the medicines use distillations. A still, or alembic, could be either elaborate or a simple pottery device and so would not necessarily figure in an inventory. There are several recipes in Grandmother Gell's collection that require the use of a still. Whilst Gervase Markham limits himself in this work to curing human ailments, this recipe collection also includes recipes for curing ailments in horses. This is a subject that Markham has covered elsewhere, so he may feel that this is more the man's sphere than the woman's.

Cookery would certainly take up a great deal of time, not to mention energy. Some tasks would be seasonal, and others daily. Whether one lived in the town or country would influence the daily work involved, and the proportion of goods purchased ready prepared. The daily meal would need to be prepared, bread would need to be baked if it was not bought in, and provisions would be laid down for future months. If an animal was slaughtered for meat, then there were sausages to make and perhaps bacon to be cured, all the parts of the animal that could be used in varying ways needed to be cooked or laid down in some way. Whilst a larder provided some measure of cold storage, most fresh foods if not eaten straight away needed considerable work and skill to preserve them. Much of this would have been unconsciously learnt as a daughter would learn much from helping her mother. It would be for the more difficult tasks that a cookery book was resorted to, or for more complex recipes.

16. Gervase Markham *The English Housewife*, edited by Michael R Best, McGill – Queen's University Press, London, 1986

The brewing of ale was part of the woman's work, although not exclusively so, and linked by the use of yeast to the baking of bread. She may also be responsible for the making of the malt for the ale, or might purchase this. That this recipe collection has no recipes for brewing ale or beer does not suggest that this was not done by the Gell family, but rather that it was such a normal part of life that no instruction was considered necessary. Hopton Hall had a Brewhouse with all the equipment necessary for brewing ale or beer. Beer or ale would be made in three strengths, strong, ordinary and 'small', the weakest sort. From the number of recipes in the collection for wines, and particularly the one that is in diary format, we know that as well as ale and beer, they were making wine and mead.

Making the reasonable assumption that a cow was kept then there was butter to be churned and cheese to be made. Huge amounts of cream were used in many of the recipes, and this would be skimmed off the milk. The necessity of keeping the dairy spotlessly clean was well known, as was the need to sterilise everything to do with dairying. Again we know that at Hopton Hall there was a dairy with all the equipment necessary for producing butter and cheese. Sweet butter was used fresh, which some recipes require, otherwise it was salted down for future use.

Gervase Markham also believes that the housewife will be skilled in producing wool, hemp, flax (linen) and cloth. He does admit that this may be sent to the dyers to be coloured. The manuscripts include a number of recipes, taken from Polygraphice[17] which give instructions on how to dye cloth in different colours, although probably not the most expensive ones as several of them are described as 'sad' colours.

Whilst Markham does not feel the need to instruct the housewife in doing her laundry, that would have been part of her duty, although she may have had someone come into the house to help her with that, if she didn't have a servant whose role it was. Household accounts of this period often have references to paying 'the woman to do the washing' and part of this payment would have been ale, as it was thirsty work. Whilst there are many theories as to how often clothes were changed and washed, we know that cleanliness was considered to be a virtue, as much because we know that its opposite, slovenliness and dirtiness, was considered a vice. There are recipes for perfumes for gloves, pomanders and for bags to put amongst clothes to keep those put away smelling fresh, as well as to deter insects which could eat the stored clothing.

17. Salmon, William, Polygraphice, London, 1681

4. The Recipe Collection

I have transcribed the recipes as they appear, adding only a little punctuation for clarity; spellings vary and are part of the charm of reading old documents. Many of the words are abbreviated in the text, and I have left these as they appear. The most common abbreviations are y for th, and the omission of vowels. Thus

w^{ch} = which w^{th} = with y^e = the

y^{or} = your y^s = this y^t = that

4.1 Made Dishes

Made dishes are the basics of a meal, the meat and fish dishes, stews and soups that would have been a part of a formal meal or for a family meal would have been the main dish. Some of them are ways of preserving meat to keep it for use in the future, such as to 'coller' various meats. Approximately a fifth of the total number of recipes are for made dishes, and of these four fifths are for meat dishes. Of the 16 for fish, six are for carp, a freshwater fish commonly eaten at this time. Anchovies are commonly used as flavouring in meat dishes, as were oysters, not at this time a luxury food, but readily available in coastal areas and particularly in London. Mrs Clay's Frigasey uses oysters and cockles. Eels were also eaten, and there are two recipes for these.

I have in places substituted other meats for veal and hare, not commonly eaten today.

6. Mead and gingerbread recipes (NA DD/E/59/56)

To make a Hodge-Podge

Take some beef & cut it in pieces as big as y^{or} hand & stew it well then take some Turneps & Carrots & cut y̅ some round, some long, some bacon, herbs, onions, parsly, capers & pepper & so stew y^{or} Turneps & herbs all together, y̅ take some butter in a sawcepan melted y̅ some flowr to make it thick so serve it up wth fry^d bread & parsly.

    12oz 300g braising steak

    8oz 225g bacon

    Turnip, carrot, onions, fresh herbs, capers

Fry the bacon, steak and onions together, add water and a large bunch of fresh herbs, a few capers, carrots and onions and stew until everything is tender.

Serve on or with bread for an authentic meal or use a stock cube and less herbs and serve with potatoes for a 21st century version.

To make Peas Soop

To 3 quarts of soft water one quart of peas & boil them till they are very tender then strain them thro a hare sive then take 3 quarters of a pound of Butter cut your bread into little Bitts & fry them then take it out and put into the pan beet mint parsly lettis a little onion & afew mary gold leaves & fry all these till they are very tender you may add salliry if you like it Season them with pepper & salt to your tast & a little sugar boile all together till they are good then put your Bread into a Dish & your Soope upon it.

    ½pt 275ml dried split peas   Mint, parsley, onion, lettuce and celery, all chopped

    3oz 75g butter

    1½pts 825ml water   Cubes of dry bread.

Soak the peas in the water for two hours before boiling, then simmer until soft. If you like a smooth soup, then liquidise this. Fry cubes of bread in half of the butter and remove from the pan. Fry the herbs etc. and stir into the soup. Serve with the fried bread croutons.

In the eighteenth century the soup would have been served on top of the bread, rather than the other way round. *'Serve on sippets'* is the phrase often used.

To make Savery baked Meat

Take an hare & bone it & take ye same quantity of fat & Leane pork & hack them very well together & after beat it very well in Mortar, then season it with pepper & Cloves & Mace & Salt, then put it in a pot to bake with a good deal of Butter & when it is tender, take out ye Gravy & fill it up with Clarified Butter.

½lb 225g diced pork	1tsp 5ml salt
½lb 225g braising steak	Butter
½tsp 7ml each of cloves, mace, pepper	

Place all the ingredients in a food processor and blend together. Transfer to a greased and lined loaf tin and dot with butter. Bake at Gas 4 350°F 180°C for 1 hour. When it is cooked, pour off the juices and allow to cool.

Note - I have substituted beef for hare, but if you wish to use rabbit please do so. This would make an interesting starter as a meat terrine, or could be served as part of a buffet.

Mrs Clay^s way to make a frigasey of Lamb, Veal, Rabits or Chickens

Cut the chickens into pieces & throw y^m into water, Let y^m Lye an hour then take y^m out & draine ye water from y^m then take a stew pan & a half a pd of fresh butter set it in the fire to melt then throw in the Chickens Let y^m stew put in some strong broth an onyon, some shred parsley, a little whole Mace, a Bunch of sweet herbs, some white wine a little vinegar, some grated Nutmeg & if you have a few oysters and cockles. Let all those stew together till the meat be enough then take 4 or 5 yolks of eggs with a little thick cream poure it into the meate sheck it over the fire till it be thick but be sure you take great care lest it curdle so serve it up with balls & sliced Lemmon pickles sippets of Bread & crisped parsley.

1½lbs 700g chicken breast	1 onion
5floz 150ml white wine	A few blades of mace
1oz 25g butter	A little fresh parsley and other fresh herbs, or 1 tsp dried mixed herbs
1tbs 15ml wine vinegar	
5floz 150ml stock	1 egg yolk
1tsp 5ml nutmeg, grated	5floz 150ml double cream

Fry the onion in a little of the butter, and remove to a plate. Melt the remaining butter and fry the chicken until cooked through. Add the stock, white wine, vinegar, herbs and spices, and the onion. Simmer for thirty minutes. Beat the egg yolk with the cream and stir into the pan, heating gently.

The 'balls' would be forced meat balls.

To make Parsnip Cakes

Take y^or parsnips w^n they are boyled break y̅ as small as you can gett y̅ & beat 6 eggs & but abt 2 or 3 of ye whites & a little Tyme & beat y̅ all together, & heat ye frying-pan very hot put y̅ in little cakes into y^or pan when they are fryed beat some butter & a little suger for ye sawce. You must put a little sugar into y^or cakes too.

2 medium sized parsnips

1 egg

Fresh thyme or rosemary

Boil the parsnips until tender and mash them with a potato masher, add the chopped herbs and beaten egg. Shape into small cakes and roll in flour. These can then either be fried in butter, until each side is golden, or cooked in the oven. I found making them into small cakes and putting them in with roast potatoes for twenty minutes worked very well.

They make an excellent accompaniment to a roast dinner, and would work very well with Christmas dinner, being a little different to roast parsnips, but are neither too rich nor tricky to make.

Scotch Collops

Take ye best part of a Leg of Veal & slice it very thin then hack it & fry it with very sweet butter & when it is fryed take Time, Winter Savory, sweet marjoram, & strip them very small, take 5 or 6 anchovies, 3 or 4 yolks of eggs beat up with a little nutmeg sliced & a whole onion, a little Broth or Gravy, put ye Liquer into ye pan & all things into y̅ pan together, then shake them well together & when you see them begin to thicken then take them from ye fire & all your meat together in your pan & put some juice of Lemmon & garnish your dish with Lemmon & Lemmon peel.

1lb 450g braising steak, bacon or veal	3 egg yolks
2oz 50g butter	Juice and peel of one lemon
1 onion	Thyme, marjoram, winter savory, chopped small
5 anchovies	5floz 150ml stock

Slice the meat thinly and beat it with a rolling pin. Fry it in the butter until cooked through then add the herbs, chopped onion and anchovies. Beat the egg yolks and add to the stock and lemon juice. Add to the pan and stir until the sauce thickens. Garnish with lemon peel and serve immediately.

Mrs Roth' weort to stew a hare

Take the hare & cut it in pieces but do not wash it then put it into a stewpan & put to it Claret & Stout as much as will Cover it, then put to it sweet marjerum, time, winter savoury, of such a sprig or two, shallot & whole pepper, a small piece of Bacon & stick it full of Cloves & Let it stew till it be tender then put to it 3 anchovies Half a p^d of Butter a Little beaten & then put in the yolks of 3 eggs, then shake them all together & when it is thick, put it into ye dish & Lay Lemmon upon it.

1lb 450g braising steak	1tsp 5ml each of peppercorns and cloves
5floz 150ml red wine	3 egg yolks
5floz 150ml Stout (or similar)	3 anchovies or 1 tsp anchovy essence
6oz 150g shallots	2oz 50g butter
Marjoram, thyme, winter savoury	Lemon slices to garnish
1 rasher bacon	

Cut the braising steak into cubes and put into a large pan with the claret and stout, herbs, peppercorns and the bacon studded with cloves. Stew gently until the meat is tender. If using anchovies, grind them to a paste in a pestle and mortar and stir into the meat. Beat the egg yolks together. Make a space in the middle of the pan if possible and melt the butter into it, then add the egg yolks. Stir it all together and heat gently until it has thickened. Transfer to a serving dish and garnish with sliced lemon.

How to Coller a pig by Mrs Clay

Take a fat pig when it is dressed, cut it up ye back & bone it, Cut of the head, throw it into water, Let it Lye all night then take it out, dry it very well with a cloth, & season it with pepper, salt, Mace, Cloves, Nutmeg, Lemmon peele & sweet herbs shred small, Strow all these in the side of ye pig & roole it up, put it in a cloth tye it at both ends boyle it in Milk & Water & Salt till it be tender & shrink from ye Cloth then tye ye Cloth cloose & hang it to coole make ye pickle of white wine & water, salt & vinegar put in whole Mace, pepper, boyle all together & when it is cold put in the pig as it is in the cloth, till you make use of it you must boyle ye head with it, & when you dish it up, set ye head at the middle. Garnish it with Greens, flower, & slices of Lemmon, You may Bone a Breast of Veale & doe it ye same way.

To stew Carp

Scale & cut y*r* Carp & wash y*e* blood out of their Bellies with vinegar, then flour them well & fry them in Butter till they are thorough hot, then put them into y*r* stewpan, with a pint of claret, two anchovies, an onion stuck with 3 or 4 cloves, 2 or 3 blades of Mace, a bunch of sweet herbs & a pound of fresh Butter, put them over a soft fire, 3 quarters of an hour will do 'em then take y*r* fish up, & put them in y*e* Dish y*u* serve them in. If y*r* sauce is not thick enough, boil it a little longer, then strain over y*r* Carp – this is a very good way to do eels, only cut them in pieces & not fry them. Garnish with horse radish & Lemon.

To hash a Calf's-head

Take the Head & boyl it when it is almost Enough take it up and cut it into little pieces then put to it some of the Broth it was boyled in and some white wine & a little onion & Bunch of sweet herbs 3 or 4 anchovies pepper half a nutmeg broken, stew all these together till it be enough then have ready Cucumber & other pickles, shread the yolks of 2 or 3 eggs beaten put these to the meat and shake them altogether over the fire y*e* may either put in the brains or dip them in the beaten yolks of eggs & fry them & lay them about the dish y*u* must boil them before y*e* fry them & you may put on Oysters & lay half a head in the middle of it or lemon round it or upon it or you may mix the brains with an egg beaten sweet herbs shread pepper salt nutmeg a little grated bread & a spoonful of cream & make them into cakes & fry them.

To Pickle Pig

Take a fat Pig & bone it & then strew on it Nutmeg cloves & mace sweet herbs & a great deal of salt. Rowle it up like Brawn a side in a Rowle boyl it till it be very tender the bones being with it then put to the Broth bay leaves Nutmeg in quarters cloves & mace & a quart of Vineagar do the Head whole and when the Broth is cold put the Pig into it so keep it for Use.

To Coller Ele

Take y*e* biggest Eles skin y⁻ & y*n* slit y*m* down y*e* back take y*e* bones & head of y⁻. Take sage, parsly, sweet marjerom shred as small as can be, Cloves, Nutmegs, Mace, & pepper finely beaten & some salt strew it over y*e* Ele & roll it up in a cloth & boyl it in Water, & Vinegar, a handful of salt & Lemon peels & a bundell of sweet herbs, keep it turning in y*e* boyling so boyl it till it be enough & hang y*or* collers on a stick till they be cold & y*or* liquor cold, then put y⁻ in to keep out y*e* wind.

To make soup called Pottage Mager without flesh

For Fridays or Wednesdays, take some Spinnage & sorrel mince it with 5 or 6 hartychoak bottoms cut in dice, wth a bunch of sweet herbs & an onion stuck with cloves put all this together into a sawcepan wth half a pound of butter set it over ye fire & keep stirring till y^e butter be melted dust a little flowr amongst it *& y^t will keep y^e butter from oyling, put 2 or 3 quarts of hot water into it & let it boyl an hour then stew some white bread (as you did y^e other [Take the bottom of two Manchets tosted very brown & hard at y^e fire & put y$^-$ into a deep dish with some of y^e same broth in y^e dish & let it boyl over a charcoal fire very softly]) wth y^e broth & so serve it up wth a whole roll of bread in y^e middle of y^e dish.

To make Bolonia Sawsages

Take a fore loyn of Pork good & fatt clean so it from all y^e skins & strings y^n shred it ye fat & lean together & to 12lb & half of meat take half a pound of salt old rich cheshire cheese grated two ounces & an ounce of pepper half an ounce of Jamaica pepper grosely beaten & an handfull of dry sage powdered. When you have mixt & wrought y^e well together put it into y^{or} large weath gutts or beef gutts well cleansed cutting y$^-$ in pieces a bout a foot long tying y$^-$ at one end wth packthread y^n put in y^e meat pressing it in very hard tye it up & hang y$^-$ not in y^e Kitchin chimney for they will be too hot they will keep a year or two w^n you use y$^-$ boyl one or more of y$^-$ (as you have occasion) for an hour & w^n they are cold cut y$^-$ in thin slices thus they have often been made in England & they have been better likt than those made in y^e City Bolonia in Italy from whence they take their name. In Italy they put in Buttock beef & beef sewet garlick & Parmasan cheese.

How to pott Beef, Veal, Venison or Hare

Take y^e hinder quarter of Veal bone it take of ye fat as is hole as you can & ye udder if it be a soe, then take ye Leane & beat it well with a rowling pinn, then take ye fat of bacon cut it in dies mix it with ye Veale, seasen it & ye fat & udder wth beaten pepper, Nutmeg & salt then put it in a pot wth a good deal of Butter att ye bottom & top, Lay ye fatt & udder upon ye meate so set it in ye oven, you may bake it wth household bread & when you draw it pour of ye butter, & take of ye fat as whole as you can then take ye meate & break it small wth your hands beat it in a mortar very small then put in the pott you designe to send to table. Lay ye meat at ye Bottom & ye fat in dies among it, settle it down well wth your hand in ye pott & when it is cold pour melted Butter over it. You must pott hares ye same way, but you must add more lard to it. And Venison is done after ye same manner only you must leave out ye lard & Nutmeg & when you come to break it wth your hands put in some of ye butter you cleared from it, & so mix it together, then putt it in your potts. Lay your fat in the middle, prefs it down wth your hand, & half an hour after put in the rest of ye Butter scalding hot yt was baked wth you must be sure to bake all your meat with a good deal of Butter if you may have enough to cover it in your pott & to mix wth the Beefe & Venison, your Beef is done ye same way wth ye Venison only you must take the Buttock piece without any fatt & beat it extremely well before & when it is baked you must wring all ye gravy out & beat it as small as dust then melt butter to mix amongst it, if you let your Beef lye in pickle four days wth salt peter & Bay Salt it will looke red, you must turn it in ye pickle & put Anchoveys in your Butter you mix amongst it it will eat & make it look like potted tounges, frothed melted butter is better to cover potts than y^t was baked wth.

22

4.2 Pyes and Tarts, savoury and sweet

Whilst the majority of our pies are round, that wasn't always the case, so many recipes refer to making a coffin for the filling. Paste, rather than pastry, is the term generally used. Often the pie would be baked with a rough pastry lid and then that would be replaced by a separately baked lid in puff paste, made in a fancy shape. If a pie dish was not used, then a free standing pie could in theory be made to any shape, and published recipe books such as Robert May *The Accomplisht Cook*[18] give drawings for suggested designs for different kinds of pies and tarts. Many of these are very elaborate and one can only imagine them being made by professional cooks in large houses. The simpler ones may well have been used more generally as the appearance of the food was considered very important. May is, however, addressing his book toward the professional cook. His parties would not be dull, he suggests for something such as a Twelfth Night celebration that *'when lifting first the lid off one pye, out skip some Frogs, which make the Ladies to skip and Shreek; next after the other pye, out come the Birds, who by natural instinct flying in the light, will put out the Candles; so what with the flying Birds and the skipping Frogs, the one above, the other beneath, will cause much delight and and pleasure to the whole company:'*

Different kinds of pastry are used for different purposes. A rough rye pastry would surround a joint of meat or be filled with meat and effectively be a pie dish and a means of keeping the meat for a long period of time. The pastry case may be formed around a wooden block, which would then be removed and the filling added. A pie funnel was used for pouring melted butter into a pie. This was used to keep the meat fresh after the juices from the meat had been poured off, as these would not keep and would spoil the rest. William Rabisha's[19] venison pie is a foot high, in either a round or square coffin, and should keep a twelvemonth if made properly. Rich puff pastry was used for tarts and pie lids, and different pastry again for making highly decorated pies. The ingredients vary but are a combination of flour, either wheat or rye, eggs, butter or suet. The section of recipes copied out by Thomas and referred to as the second book start with a selection of recipes for paste, including one for puff paste very similar to those that many of us will remember making at school but may not have made very often since. Given the grouping they may have been taken from a published cookery book, but are attributed to Mrs Billings and Mrs Gallimore. Pastry cases may be baked blind for custards, with instructions such as *'harden y^{or} coffins in ye oven'* and when the filling is such as a custard or cheesecake mix then you fill your coffins at the oven.

To make Past for Tarts

Take 3 pound & a half of flower put to it half a pound of butter when ye liquor boyls put in ye butter y^n make y^{or} past indifferent stiff.

18. Robert May *The Accomplisht Cook,* London, 1685
19. William Rabisha, *The whole body of Cookery dissected,* London, 1682

To make past for all sorts of g^d pyes

Take 14 pound of flour put to it 4 yolks of Eggs yⁿ make your liquor boyl & put in half a pound of clarified suet & a pound & a half of butter boyl'd in ye liquor, yⁿ make ye past indifferent stiff.

To make Puff Past

Take 3 pound & half of flour put to it 8 whites of eggs & one yolk make it into a past with cold water & roll in a pound & a half of butter at 9 or 10 times & give it a small coat of flowr betwixt every rolling.

To make Past for Cheesecakes

Take 3 pound of flour, put to it half a pound of butter rubb ye butter in ye flour & put in 2 yolks of eggs & make y^{or} liquor boyl very well & let it stand untill it be almost cold yⁿ make ye past very stiff.

To make Past for Custards

Take 3 pound of flower put to it 3 yolks of eggs yⁿ make it into a past very stiff wth boyling liquor without butter.

To make an Apple Pudding [Tart]

Take some Apples & scald 'em, they shou'd be good & quick tasted, take 3 quarter of a pound of pulp, to which add 8 eggs, leave out half the whites, half a p^d of single refin'd Sugar beat with the Eggs, Grater the peel, & squeeze in the Juce, of one Good Limon, to which add half a p^d of Melted Butter, it must be the last thing just before it goes to the Oven put a sheet of thin past in the Dish.

6oz 150g apples, cooked and puréed

Juice and rind of 1 lemon

4 eggs, but only 3 whites

Line an 8 in 20 cm round baking tin with shortcrust pastry. Mix together the apple purée, eggs, sugar and juice and rind of the lemon. Stir in the melted butter and bake at Gas 5 375°F 190°C for approximately an hour.

Note – I have halved the quantity of butter in the filling, so that it is not as rich as the original.

The Second book

1 To make Past for Tarts
or mince pyes

Take 3 pound & a half of flower put
to it half a pound of butter when y^e
liquor boyls put in ye butter y^n make yor past
indifferent stiff.

2 To make past for all sorts of g^t pyes.

Take 4 pound of flour put to it 4 yolks of
eggs y^n make your liquor boyl & put in half
a pound of clarified suet & a pound & a half
of butter boyl'd in ye liquor, y^n make ye past
indifferent stiff.

3 To make Puff past.

Take 3 pound & half of flour putt to it 3
whites of eggs & one yolk make it into a past
wth cold water & roll in a pound & a half of
butter at 9 or 10 times & give it a small coat of
flour betwixt every rolling.

4 To make Past for Cheesecakes

Take 3 pound of flour, put to it half a pound
of butter rubb ye butter in y^r flour & put in
2 yolks of eggs & make yor liquor boyl very
well & let it stand untill it be almost cold y^n make
ye past very stiff.

5 To make past for Custards.

Take 3 pound of flower put to it 3 yolks
of eggs y^n make it into a past very stiff wth boyling liquor without butter.

To bake Wardens or quinces[20]

Pare y̅ & core y̅ᵐ & cut y̅ᵉ sharp ends flat & boyl y̅ᵐ in white wine & sugar untill y̅ syrrup grow thick then lay y̅ out to coole & make a coffin for y̅ of tough thick past lay y̅ in & stick whole cloves & cinnamon in y̅, put in sugar & some of y̅ syrrup they were boyled in, close y̅ᵉ pye & bake it moderately.

1½lb 700g baking apples	3oz 75g sugar
5floz 150ml white wine	A few cloves and a little broken cinnamon stick

Peel and core the apples and cut them into quarters, poach them gently in the wine and sugar. Line an 8in 20cm pie plate with shortcrust pastry. Fill with the apple mixture and scatter the cloves and cinnamon on. Cover with the remaining pastry and cook at Gas Mark 6, 400°F, 200°C for 30 minutes, until the pastry is golden. Serve hot or cold.

To make minc'd pyes

Take 2 Tongues the same weight in Beef Suit 4 pound of Currans and 2 of Raisins, half an Ounce of Nutmeggs, a quarter of an Ounce of Mace, half a quarter of an ounce of Cloves and Cinnamen and D° of Lemon Peel, Wine, Brandy and Sugar to your taste. The bigness of the Tongues must be considered when you put in the above nam'd Spices &c.

6oz 150g cooked sliced tongue	½tsp 2.5ml each of cloves and cinnamon, ground
6oz 150g suet	
6oz 150g currants	Grated rind of one lemon
3oz 75g raisins	2tbsp 30ml brandy
2tsp 10ml nutmeg, grated	4oz 100g dark brown sugar
1tsp 5ml mace, ground	

Cut the sliced tongue into small pieces and mix all the ingredients together. Line a round 8inch 20cm pie dish with shortcrust pastry and fill and cover. Bake at Gas Mark 6 400°F 200°C for 30 - 40 minutes. Serve hot or cold.

One of two recipes in the collection for minc'd pyes, these or something very similar would have been eaten at each of the meals in the menu plans. It works well when served with mulled wine as something that is neither savoury or sweet.

20. Wardens are winter cooking pears but the recipe works well with apples too. The quince is the English quince which grows as a tree rather than the ornamental Chaenomeles.

To season a Chicken Pye

Bruise ye bones of some & joynt ye rest season y^m wth cloves, mace, nutmeg, & pepper, salt & some sliced lemon not ye peel fill ye pye & put in butter close it & bake it, when it is baked dissolve 2 anchovies in white wine & so put it into ye pye hot.

1lb 450g chicken breasts	2 anchovies
5floz 150ml white wine	1oz 25g butter
½tsp 2.5ml each of ground cloves, mace, nutmeg and pepper	½ lemon sliced, or 1tbsp 15ml lemon juice

Fry the chicken breasts until cooked through and then add the spices and lemon. Put into an 8 in 20 cm pie tin lined with short crust pastry and dot with the butter. Cover with pastry, make slits in the top and bake at Gas 6 400°F 200°C for 30 minutes until the pastry is golden. Mash the anchovies in a pestle and mortar and add them to the wine, or liquidise the anchovies in the wine. If serving the pie hot, heat the wine mixture first and then pour it through the slits in the pastry. Serve hot or cold.

4.3 Puddings, savoury and sweet

Puddings, *'blessed be he who invented pudding'* is a complimentary comment from a Frenchman called Misson, writing in the 1690s when visiting England. Puddings were both savoury or sweet, baked or boiled. Many of the savoury puddings we would now think of as stuffings, but puddings included dumplings, blood puddings, batter puddings, and pancakes. The sweet puddings in this collection are often very simply titled; 'a good pudding', 'a six hour pudding', 'plum pudding'. The pudding cloth started to be used in the seventeenth century, before then boiled puddings were cooked in a gut of some sort. They could be made with flour or breadcrumbs, cream and eggs, and, of course suet. Whilst they sound very fatty, they are surprisingly light – as much of the fat is lost during the boiling process. They are rich and warming, spiced with mace, cloves, ginger, cinnamon, nutmeg, and rosewater, or orange flower water.

Baked puddings could be rice based, fruit, or creams. They would be served with a sauce – 'the sauce for this is butter, sugar and sack' is a frequent comment at the end of a recipe– again, something else that tastes better than it sounds. For gentle heating, a chaffing dish would be used. A 'hasty pudding', was made using milk or cream, thickened with flour, breadcrumbs or oatmeal and cooked in a pan over the fire or on a stove. They could be served simply as they were, or were a stage in the cooking of a more complex recipe.

Cooking notes

The boiled puddings are designed to be boiled in a gut or cloth, if you try and use a pudding basin they really don't work, and all you will get is a fatty mess. To use a cloth, take a generous square of muslin, first butter it fairly thickly, and then sprinkle a little flour on it. If the pudding mix is quite sloppy it is easiest to put the cloth into a bowl to keep the shape until it is tied up. Leave a little space for it to swell when you tie it up. Vegetarians can happily use vegetarian suet, and reduced fat suet works well too.

or one good Mess of verjuice to make
it quail, yn wth it is fully quailed, cast it as thin
as you can upon a fair Cupboard cloth & as
softly as you can yt ye water may draine away
& so shift it into a dry cloth & let it hang
all night & when it is stiff wch will be ye next
day season it up wth sugar, rosewater, & a little
saffron & so dish it to ye board.

82. To make Puffs

Take a pint of cheese curds, drain ym dry bruise
ym small with your hand & put in two ——
handful of flour a little sugar, 3 or 4
yolks of Eggs a little nutmeg & salt, mingle
these together & make ym in little lumps
like eggs, fry ym in fresh butter, serve ym up
wth a little fresh butter & sugar.

83. A Custard

Take a quart of good Cream ye yolks
of half a dozen Eggs ye crum of a manchet
shredd dates Currans washt & pickt a little
Muskadell & rosewater

Finis primi Libri.

from Mrs Mason

p̃ me   Thomam Gell

8. Last page of first book copied out by Thomas Gell (NA DD/E/59/58)

To make a Carrot Pudding

Take 2 large Carrots grater them then take one quart of Cream or new milk and slice 2 penny Loaves into the milk then put to them 6 Eggs well beaten half a pound of Sugar half a pound of melted Buter & a whole Nuttmeg graterd mix all these together & immediately set it into a quick oven and when it is drawn pour melted Butter into it and if you will please me a good deal of that Liquor folks call Sack upon it then pray Eat it while it is hot But don't Burn yͤ*.*

1 large carrot	4oz 100g butter, melted
3 eggs	½ a nutmeg, grated
1pt 600ml cream or milk	A little wine or brandy, or serve with a brandy sauce.
4oz 100g sugar	
12oz 300g breadcrumbs	

Combine all the ingredients apart from the wine together and put in a casserole dish with a lid. Bake at Gas 5 375°F 190°C for 45 minutes, then remove the lid and cook for approximately half an hour. Pour a little wine or brandy over the top and serve with cream, or serve with custard or a brandy sauce.

This quantity of nutmeg gives a quite distinctive flavour, use a little less if you prefer. I use half a pint each of cream and milk for this recipe.

To make a 6 hourˢ Pudding

Take raisins one pd pick yͫ & stone yͫ Beefe Suet shred very fine & small & yͤ cleanest one pd 6 eggs well beaten, of the finest flower 3 spoonfulls, cream 3 spoonfulls, one nutmeg, salt it according to your tast mix them well together & tye yͫ up pretty close in a cloth & keep it continuously boyling for 6 hours you must serve it up with sack butter & sugar note when you put water in the boyling to it must be boyling water out of some other skillet because it must not be hindred.

8oz 225g raisins	1½ tbsp 25ml cream
6oz 150g suet	3oz 75g flour
3 eggs	

Mix all ingredients together and put into a greased and floured pudding cloth. Tie up and boil for three hours, topping the water up as required. Halving the original quantities also halves the cooking time.

For the Sauce

Heat 2oz 50g butter and the same of sugar with a little wine and pour over.

To make a good pudding

Take a penny loaf grate it & put to it as much boild Cream to it as will soak it take Beef Suit shred very fine twelve eggs 4 of the Whites a grated Nutmeg sweeten it to you tast put in as many Currains as you please.

12oz 300g breadcrumbs	6 eggs
6oz 150g suet	2tsp 10ml nutmeg, grated
½pt 300ml cream	6oz 150g currants

Heat the cream to just below boiling point and stir in the breadcrumbs. It will make a thick mixture. Take it off the heat and stir in the beaten eggs, nutmeg and currants. Put into a greased and floured pudding cloth and boil for 2 hours. This could be served with the same sauce as the '6 hour' pudding.

To stew Apples to colour y^m

Pare q^rter & core y & put y into a skillet & put to y^m a little rosewater & a little fair water some lemon peel minced fine, 3 or 4 cloves, some whole cinnamon, keep these stirring over a clear quick fire untill they grow very thick & sweeten y^m wth sugar y^n you may colour y red wth scutchionele[21] bruised & tied in a clout, & dip it in water & strain it upon ye apples, to make y^m yellow take saffron & use it ye same way, for green take ye juice of spinage & mix wth y^m.

1lb 450g cooking apples	3 cloves
1tsp 5ml rose water	Small piece of cinnamon stick
Zest of 1 lemon	A little sugar
1 tbsp 15ml water	

Cook the apples with the water, rose water and spice until they are soft. For a yellow colour, pour boiling water on to a little saffron and then add the coloured water to the apples. Sugar to taste.

This makes a very nice spiced apple filling for a pie or crumble, or serve as apple sauce with pork.

21. Cochineal

An Oatmeal Pudding

Take a handful of small oatmeal a Pint of Milk thicken it over the fire, till it be like a Pudding, then take it off the fire & stirr in a pound of Beef Suet shread very small, or butter, then take 2 Neaple biskets graterd very fine & 6 Eggs leaving out 2 of the whites, beat your Eggs with 2 or 3 spoonfuls of Sack & a little salt, Grater in almost half a Nutmeg & as much Sugar as will sweeten it, stir it together so put it into your dish, it will take about 3 quarters of an Hour bakeing, you must butter yᵉ bottom of your Dish, you may put in a little Rosewater if you please.

½pint 300ml milk

1oz 25g oatmeal

4oz 100g butter

2 eggs

6 trifle sponge fingers, crumbled

1tbsp 15ml sherry

1tsp 5ml nutmeg

Stir the oatmeal into the milk in a saucepan and heat gently until it comes to the boil and thickens somewhat. Remove from the heat and stir in the butter which will melt, and then the crumbs from the trifle sponges and the nutmeg, at which point it will become very thick. Beat the eggs and add the sherry to them. Gradually beat the eggs into the oatmeal mixture. Pour into a buttered casserole dish, and sprinkle a little more nutmeg on top. Bake at Gas 3 325°F 170° C for 45 minutes.

In no way akin to porridge, despite the use of oatmeal, this makes a rich dessert dish. The amount of butter used in this recipe has been halved, and it could still be reduced down to a couple of ounces without spoiling the recipe.

To make a White Bread Pudding

Take a pint of milk or cream, when it Boils Thicken it with a penny loaf grater'd take it off the fire and stir in 3 quarters of a pound of Butter, 6 eggs a Nutmegg, orange flower-water wine and sugar to your taste.

1pint 600ml cream

12oz 300g breadcrumbs

8oz 200g butter

6 eggs

1tsp 5ml orange flower water or rose water

½ nutmeg, grated

2oz 50g sugar

2tbsp 30ml wine or sherry

Heat the cream gently to boiling point and then stir the breadcrumbs in, cooking it until it thickens. Add the butter, beaten eggs, nutmeg, wine and flower water and mix well. Place in a pudding cloth and boil for two hours.

To make a Pippin Pudding

Take 4 or 5 good pippins more or less as your dish requires, pare them, then cut off the top & scrape all the core out & not break the apple, scrape a good deal out, then butter your dish very well & stick your apples in the butter that they may not swimm, then take a pint of sweet cream & 6 yolks of eggs well beaten together & grate two or three good bisketts with nutmeg & sugar, a little sack, what sweet meats you please, so fill your apples & pour the rest all over your dish, your top of your apples will be a little above your stuffing, so bake it with care, stick it with Lemmon & sittern, put past about your dish.

1lb 450g cooking apples, peeled, cored and sliced

1oz 25g butter

6 trifle sponge fingers, broken into small pieces

½pt 300ml cream

3 egg yolks

2tbsp 30ml sherry

2oz 50g raisins

1oz 25g sugar

1tsp 5ml nutmeg, grated

Spread the butter over the bottom of a pie dish and put half the apples in a layer over it. Beat the egg yolks into the cream, and mix the sponge fingers, nutmeg and raisins into it. Put the more solid part of this mixture on top of the layer of apples and then spread the remaining apple in a layer above this. Pour the rest of the cream mixture on and cover with pastry. Bake at Gas 6 400°F 200°C for 20 minutes, and then reduce the temperature to Gas 4 350°F 180°C and bake for another 20 minutes

This recipe has been altered a little to produce something on a smaller scale than the original version, although the essence of the recipe is still there. It is delicious either hot or cold. You could serve with more cream, or with custard.

To make Lemon Creame

Take a pint of sweet cream & ye juice of two lemons squeese ye into a bason, & put as much sugar to ye juice as will make it very thick, then warm y^{or} cream & put it in by spoonfulls into y^{or} juice stirring it till it be all in, so dish it.

1pt 600ml cream	Sugar to taste
Juice of 2 lemons	

Heat the lemon juice to dissolve the sugar, and then gently warm the cream and stir it into the lemon mixture gradually.

This will give a very rich lemon flavoured cream which could be served with something light, such as a fruit salad, or with shortbread and fruit. Alternatively it could have sugar sprinkled on top and be served as a lemon crème brulée. There are no less than six recipes in the collection for lemon cream, of which this is the simplest to make. All the other recipes use eggs. This one is very effective though, as the acidity of the lemon sets the cream.

The best sort of Lemon Cream

Take 4 great Lemons pare ye Rind of very thin & let it steep 2 or 3 hours in a pint of fair water, then take out y^{or} rind & wring in ye juice of y^{or} lemons, beat ye whites of 8 eggs & one yolk & put to it, sweeten it to your tast wth double refined sugar & put in 2 or 3 spoonfulls of orange flower water & a little ambergrise, strain it into a silver bason, set it on ye fire, let it scald but not boyle till it be pretty thick, keep it stirring all ye while tis on ye fire, then take it of & keep stirring till it be cold.

This recipe is representative of the other lemon cream recipes in the collection.

To make jumbled Sillibubs

To half a pint of wine, put a pint of cream, sugare & lemon peel to your taste, Jumble 'em or mill 'em well with a Chocolate mill & pour 'em into y^r glasses.

5floz 150ml white wine	10floz 300ml double cream
3oz 75g sugar	Grated rind of 1 lemon

Whisk all the ingredients together well, and transfer to wine glasses to serve. For an authentic decoration, use either lemon zest, or candied rose or violet petals.

This will easily serve six, as it is very rich.

To make a Sillibub

Fill half yor sillibub pot wth Syder or white wine put in good store of Sugar & some nutmeg & slice it well together & when ye sugar is melted put in thick cream by 2 or 3 spoonfull at a time as hard as you can as though you milked it in & stirr it together very softly round about then let it stand at least two hours before you eat it for standing makes it curd.

5floz 150ml white wine	10floz 300ml double cream
2oz 50g sugar	1tsp 5ml nutmeg, ground

Dissolve the sugar in the wine and mix in the nutmeg, and then pour the cream in from as great a height as possible. Stir it together very gently and leave to set in the fridge. You will get an almost blancmange texture floating on the wine.

Syllabubs could be made by milking straight from the cow into the wine or cider, which this method emulates. The acidity of the wine acts in a similar way to rennet in the cream. Again this is a very rich dessert.

A Rice Pudding

Take a pint of cream & a q^r of Pound of Rice Flower make a hasty pudding take it off the fire, stirr in 3 q^{rs} of a pound of butter beaten well, & put them thro a hair sieve put sugar to your taste cinnamon and Mace beaten a little sack and Rosewater stirr all together & put it in a buttered dish & stick in some orange Lemon or Cittern peel half an hour will bake it.

1pt 600ml milk	½tsp 2.5ml each cinnamon and mace
4oz 100g ground rice	2tbsp 30ml white wine
8oz 200g butter	1tsp 5ml rose water
2oz 50g sugar	Lemon peel

Heat the milk and stir the ground rice into it, continuing to heat until it thickens. Remove from the heat and stir in the butter, which will melt, and the other ingredients. Transfer to a casserole dish and bake in the oven at Gas 4 350°F 180°C for 30 minutes.

I have reduced the butter and substituted milk for the cream in this recipe. An alternative to using ground rice would be to use pudding rice, omit heating the milk, and simply to stir all the ingredients together and bake at Gas 2 300°F 150°C for two hours.

To make a Hagust pudding

Take a pound of greats[22] steep y͏ᵉ all night in a quart of new milk y͏ⁿ take a pound & half of beef sewet shred small very small y͏ⁿ take 3 handfull of sweet herbs shred small 3 q͏ʳᵗᵉʳˢ of a pound of currants 3 eggs & a halfpenny loaf grated, a little cloves, & mace beaten small & a little salt, stirr y͏ᵉ all together & put y͏ᵉ into ye Maw of a sheep being washed very clean & laid in water y͏ᵉ night before, then sow it & if y͏ᵉ Maw be thin lie it in a strainer & put it into a pot when y͏ᵉ pot boyles let it boyl gently 2 hours.

4oz 100g oatmeal		1 egg	
10floz 300ml milk		3oz 75g breadcrumbs	
6oz 150g suet		1tsp 5ml cloves, ground	
3oz 75g currants		½tsp 2.5ml mace, ground	

Soak the oatmeal in the milk for at least two hours. Stir the rest of the ingredients into the milk and oatmeal and mix well together. Put into a pudding cloth and tie securely, and boil for around two hours.

When I made this I omitted the herbs and served it as a sweet pudding. One presumes that it gets its name from the sheep's maw, which the dish we know as haggis is usually cooked in, rather than the ingredients.

To make calves foot Jelly

To 4 calf's-feet take a gallon of fair water, cut y͏ᵐ in pieces, put y͏ᵐ in a pipkin close cover'd, & boil y͏ᵐ softly till almost half be consum'd; then run it thro a Sieve & let it stand till it be cold, then take off y͏ᵉ Fat top & bottom, y͏ᵉ fine part of y͏ᵉ Jelly melt in a preserving pan, & put in a pint Rhenish-wine, y͏ᵉ Juice of 4 or 5 lemons double refin'd sugar to y͏ᵉ taste y͏ᵉ whites of 8 eggs beaten to a froth, stir & boil all these together near half an hour then strain it thro a sieve, into a Jelly bag put into y͏ᵉ bag a sprig of Rosemary & a piece of Lemon-peel, pass it thro y͏ᵉ bag till tis as clear as water, y͏ᵘ may cut some peel like threads & put in half y͏ᵉ glasses.

To make Almond Puddings

Take a pound of almonds very finely beaten mingle with a quart of cream 4 penny loaves grated 10 eggs half a pound of beef sewet shred small y͏ᵉ marrow of two bones shred small half a pound of sugar or better, cloves & mace w͏ᵗ you think fit, 2 nutmegs, half a q͏ʳᵗᵉʳ of a pint of rosewater, a little salt a little musk & Ambergrese mingle all these together & put y͏ᵉ into guts, fill y͏ᵉ not too full & so boyl y͏ᵉ, when you take y͏ᵉ up let y͏ᵉ lye on one side y͏ⁿ turn y͏ᵉ on y͏ᵉ other before they be cold.

An excellent example of how puddings were cooked before the use of pudding cloths. Musk and Ambergrice were very popular 16th and 17th century ingredients, pointing to a quite early date for this recipe.

A Tansy Pudding

Take a pint of cream, 8 eggs, leaving out 4 whites, thicken y^r cream with three parts of a penny Loaf Grated, & 2 large Biskets, green it with ye juce of Spinnage, juce of Tansy & Sugar to taste, then stir into it a quarter of a pound of Butter. Garnish with Orange.

A Quaking Pudden

Take a pint of cream 4 yolks & 2 white beaten a spoonfull of flower sugar & spice & salt to y^{or} tast you must boyl y^e spice in y^e milk in a bagg yⁿ when it is cold add y^e eggs & Rosewater.

To make good Pan=cakes

Take a quart of Cream, 8 Eggs without y^e whites, beat them very well together then put in a handful of fine flower, & a pound of melted butter, then beat them well together & so bake them.

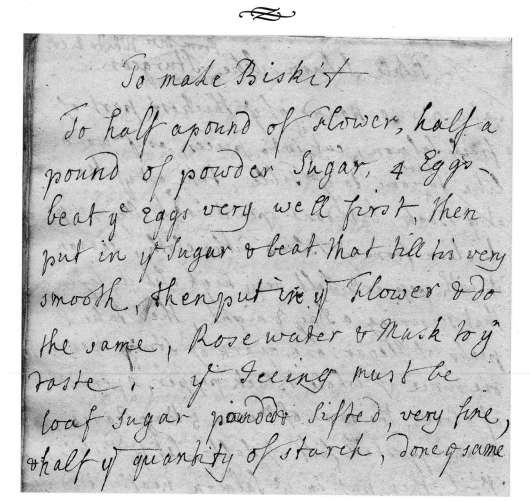

9. Example of a 'Biskit' recipe (NA DD/E/59/56)

To make Quince Marmaylett.

Take a pound of sugar beaten & put as much water to it as will something more than wett it, then sett it on ye fire & scumm it, then take a pound of Quinces when they are cor... & paired & put them in your sirrup & let them boyl very leasurely being covered, then take a quart of water & put into it your cores & pairings & let them boyl till it be very strong, then strain out almost half a pint of that water & put to your Quinces & let them boyl leasurely till they are tender & look of a good colour, then take them up out of ye sirrup & break them small with a spoon in a Porringer, & when you think it is small enough, put it into your sirrup again & boyl it a little longer & so glaze it up; Your Quinces must boyl but a very little while on ye sirrup before your water that boyled the cores in.

For Ordinary Wiggs.

Take a Peck of Flower, two pound of fresh butter, melt your butter in 3 pints of new milk over a soft fire, take a quart of ale Yest, 6 eggs, 2 ounces of Carroway seeds unbruised one ounce of Coriander seed beaten & sifted, a pound of sugar, mix all these together & let it stand by ye fire half an hour, add to it a quarter of an ounce of Cloves and mace & a Nutmeg & so bake them in a quick Oven.

To make a Water for ye Eyes.

Take 2 Drams of fine Bole Armoniack 2 Drams of Copperice, 1 dram of white Camphir all finely powdered, sett 2 quarts of spring water over ye fire till it is ready to boyl, then put it into an earthen pan & put in ye powders & stir all together till it is quite cold, & then bottle it up for use.

Elder Berry Wine.

Take 20 pound of Malago Razons & rubb them clean & chopp them small boyl 5 Gallons of water one hour, then pour it hot upon them & let it stand 10 days stirring it 2 or 3 times a day, then strain it out & put into it 6 pints of ye Juice of Elder berrys which must be boyled in an Earthen pot for 3 or 4 hours set in a kettle of water but so that the water may not touch ye Berrys, & when boyled enough strain ye Juice from them & when cold put it to ye other Liquour, & stir it well together, then tunn it & lett it stand 6 weeks or more as you see occasion & then bottle it for use.

Spirit of Elder.

Take a good quantity of Elder Berrys full ripe & press out ye Juice, then tun up this Juice & keep it till Xmas then distill it in an Alembick.

Elder Water.

Take Elder berrys & bruise them & sett them to work with Yest, & lett them work 8 or 9 days then still them in an Alembick, they must be covered whilst working with a woolen Cloath.

To make Lemmon Bisketts.

Take half a pound of Almonds, blanch them in cold water, beat them very fine, with ye froth of ye Whites of 6 Eggs whipt to a froth & a spoonfull of sweet water take a pound of double refined sugar beaten & sifted fine & a quarter of pound of fine flower, grate in ye Peel of 2 large Lemmons & mix it with ye Yolks of six eggs, mix all well together, butter ye Pans just as you put them into ye Oven sift some sugar over them, you may put in a very little juice of Lemmon.

10. Marmaylett and Wigg recipes from those written on accounts paper (NA DD/E/59/57)

37

4.4 Breads, Cakes and Bisketts

The largest group of recipes in the collection are a variety of bread, cake and biscuit recipes. Cakes and biscuits were originally eaten with ale, either as a snack, as breakfast, or as supper. They would often be given or purchased as refreshments for travellers, or might be served at a gathering such as a funeral. Wiggs would particularly be used in this way, they are made from an enriched dough flavoured with caraway, and in some areas could have been served with cheese as well. It may be what workers were given as part of their recompense for harvest work. They could be made at home, and the variety of recipes in this collection suggests that they often were in the Gell household, or they could also be purchased from the bakers.

The cake recipes are often for huge quantities. Whilst fruit cakes predominate they are not the very rich, heavily fruited versions that we use as wedding or Christmas cakes, but far nearer to a fruit bread, which does to some extent explain what seem to be very short cooking times for the quantities involved. Yeast would have been in liquid form as 'ale barm', so an appropriate liquid has been substituted to give the correct consistency to the mixtures.

The majority of these cakes and biscuits keep very well, but the cakes in particular are much drier than we are used to. Eating dry bread is something we have become unused to, but as it was often served with a pottage, that would not have been a problem, and the cakes were generally served with ale, into which they could, and would, be dunked.

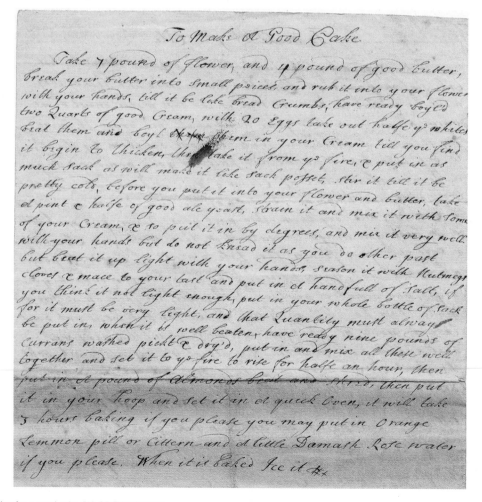

11. Second recipe for a good cake (NA DD/E/59/57/43)

Recipe notes.

Flour is plain unless stated otherwise.

Butter is preferable to margarine, it gives an authentic rich flavour and in many of the recipes that use less sugar than we are used to, this is important. Those concerned about cholesterol can substitute appropriately. The quantities produced by these recipes have been reduced in most cases.

To make breakfast cakes

Take 4 pounds of flower a pint of milk & 3 eggs half a pound of butter 5 spoonfulls of good east a little salt melt the butter in the milk but don't let the milk be too warm when you mix the cakes mix the milk eggs east & salt all togeather then put in the flower and beat it well with your hand Set it to the fire half an hour to rise role them pritty thin and make them in a quick oven.

1lb 450g strong plain flour (see note below)	1 egg
½ level tsp 5ml salt	2oz 50g butter
5floz 125ml milk	½oz 10g fresh yeast or a 7g sachet of dried yeast

Warm the milk and melt the butter. Combine these and blend in the fresh yeast if using, or stir the dried yeast into the flour with the salt. Add the milk, butter, egg and knead to a smooth dough. Leave to rise in a warm place for half an hour, then knock it back, roll out and using a plain cutter cut into rounds. Cook at Gas 6 400°F 200°C for approximately 15 minutes.

Using plain rather than strong plain flour will give a heavier texture but would be nearer to the eighteenth century texture. A mixture of half white and half wholemeal flour works well for these.

Another sort of Cakes

Take 2 quarts of good Milk 6 Eggs 6 Spoonfulls of East a little Salt beat the Eggs well warm the milk mix them all together put in flower to make It a thin Batter set It to the fire an hour to rise bake them upon a Cake stone over the fire.

1 pint 600ml milk	1lb 4oz 575g flour
1 egg	1oz 20g fresh yeast or a 7g sachet of dried yeast

Warm the milk to blood heat and stir in the fresh yeast if using, or add the dried yeast to the flour. Beat the egg into the milk to make a batter. Leave to rise for an hour. You will get a very bubbly sticky mixture. Stir. Heat a griddle and melt a little butter on it, drop spoonfuls of batter on it and let them cook gently until the underneath is golden brown and the edges have dried. Flip them over and cook the other side.

These are delicious served warm with jam or honey, but would have been used as a quick alternative to bread.

To make Wiggs – this is good

Take 2 pound of flower and one half pound to dredge with 5 ounce of Butter rub it into yr flower a pint & half of milk new milk warm mix half a pint of barm and the milk together put it into your past mix it well then set it to the fire to rise then put in half a pound of 5 penny sugar half an ounce of Carraway seeds beat it till it leaves your hand butter your tins and lay em on set them to the fire to rise then bake them.

1lb 450g flour
plus a generous amount for kneading

2½ oz 60g butter

¾ pt 450ml milk

1oz 25g fresh yeast or a 7g sachet of dried yeast

4oz 100g sugar

2tsp 10ml caraway seeds

Stir the dry ingredients together including the dried yeast if using. Rub the butter into the flour. Warm the milk and blend in the fresh yeast if using. Mix well to make a dough. The dough will be quite sticky at this stage. Leave to rise for 30 minutes. Turn out and knead with the extra flour and then shape into rolls. Place on a greased baking sheet and bake at Gas 7 425°F 230°C for approximately 15 minutes.

Gingerbread

Take 2 Quarts of Flower & a quarter & half of Butter & rub it in the flower, one Pound & half of Treacle & qur & half of Brown Sugar, Ginger & Carraway Seeds of each half an ounce Candied Limon one ounce & half & lay it upon Wafer Paper.

12oz 350g flour

6oz 175g brown sugar

8oz 225g butter

2tbsp 30ml ginger

12oz 175g treacle

1tsp 15ml caraway seeds

Candied peel (optional)

Rub the butter into the flour and sugar, stir in the ginger and caraway, then form a soft dough with the treacle. Roll out and cut into rounds or whatever shape you prefer, bake on a tray at Gas 4 350°F 180°C for 10-15 minutes.

Gingerbread had changed from a very hard, almost confection in Tudor times, to something still very hard and strong flavoured, but closer to the modern version. These could be made using moulds. They would also be purchased at fairs, as well as made within the home.

Sugar Cakes

Take 8 ounce of Sugar beat it fine & dry it work it into half a pound of Sweet Butter but first wash the Butter in a little Rose-water then beat the yolks of 3 Eggs & put them into the Butter & Sugar with a pound of fine flower work them well together then rowl it out thin & cut it with glasses & prick y^m full of holes so bake them in a Soft Oven, a quarter of an hour will bake 'em.

8oz 225g sugar	1lb 450g flour
8oz 225g butter	1tsp 15ml rosewater
3 egg yolks	

Cream the butter and sugar together, add the egg yolks and rosewater, then mix in the flour. It will make quite a crumbly mix. Roll it out and cut into rounds. Bake at Gas 4 350°F 180°C for approximately 15 minutes until they are a pale straw colour.

If you cannot get hold of rosewater you could use vanilla essence for a less authentic but tasty alternative. Using a glass to cut them out dispenses with the need for a biscuit cutter.

To make Shrewsbury Cakes

Take to one pound of sugar 3 pound of ye finest flour one nutmeg a little cinamunt ye sugar & spices must be pound & sifted, 3 eggs, so much butter as wth a good temporing will bring it to a good past y^n mould it & roll it & cut y^m into w^t bigness you please, prick y^-.

1lb 450g flour	8oz 225g butter
5oz 100g sugar	1tsp 5ml ground nutmeg
1 egg	1tsp 5ml cinnamon

Mix the dry ingredients together and then rub in the butter. Mix to a paste with the egg. Roll out and cut into rounds. Prick them and bake at Gas 4 350°F 180°C for 12 – 15 minutes.

To make French Rolls

Take 2 quarts of milk a quarter of a pound of butter the Whites of 5 eggs a pint of good east a little salt Rub the Butter well in the Flower beat the eggs well, warm the Milk and put in the eggs & east & salt & make it into a very light paste beat it very well with your hand let it stand half an hour by the fire side to rise, make them into little cakes and bake them upon tins in a quick oven.

1pint 600ml milk	1tsp 5ml salt
1oz 25g butter	1oz 25g fresh yeast or a 7g sachet of dried yeast
2 egg whites	2lb 900g strong plain flour

Heat the milk to blood temperature and if using fresh yeast, blend this in. If using dried yeast stir this into the flour with the salt. Rub the butter into the flour, mix to a dough with the milk and knead well. Leave to rise until doubled in size and then shape into 16 large rolls. Bake at Gas 7 425°F 220°C for 15-20 minutes.

To make Jumballs

Take 3 qrters of flour, fine sugar half a^{lb}, fresh butter a qrte, 2 yolks & one white of eggs, 2 spoonfull of rosewater & a few caraway seeds & so bake y- in a drying oven.

8oz 225g flour	2tsp 10ml rosewater
1 egg	4oz 100g butter
4oz 100g sugar	1tsp 5ml caraway seeds

Mix all the ingredients together and turn out onto a well floured board. Roll into a sausage shape and cut into 12 equal lengths. Shape these into knot shapes and place on a baking tray. Bake at Gas 4 350°F 180°C for 20 minutes.

Whilst this particular recipe does not specify shaping the biscuits Jumballs were usually knot shaped, and this would be taken as understood in writing the recipe down.

To make Craknets

Take half a pound of fine flowr dried & as much fine sugar searced mixt with a spoonful of Coriander seed bruised, & 2 ounces of butter melted amongst yᵉ flowr & sugar wet it with yᵉ yolks of two eggs, half a spoonfull of rosewater & two spoonfull of cream or as will wet it work yᵉ past till it be soft & limber to roll & work, then roll it very thin & cut it round by little plates lay yᵐ upon buttered papers & when they go into yᵉ oven prick yᵐ & wash yᵉ tops of them yᵉ yolk of an egg beaten & made thin with rosewater or fair water they will ungive with keeping therefore before they are eaten they must be dried in a warm oven to make yᵐ crisp.

8oz 225g flour	1tsp 5ml coriander seed, crushed
2oz 50g butter, melted	1tsp 5ml rosewater
8oz 225g sugar	4tbs 60ml cream
2 yolks of eggs	Extra egg yolk to brush if desired.

Mix all the ingredients together well, and roll out thinly. Cut them into circles and place on a well greased baking tray. Brush with egg yolk mixed with water and a little rosewater if desired, prick them and bake at Gas 5 375°F 190°C for 10 to 15 minutes, until tinged gold. They will go soft with keeping, so can be crisped up again by putting in a warm oven for a few minutes.

This recipe comes from Robert May, *The Accomplist Cook*[23].

To make a Cake

Break 6 eggs into a pan & put into it a pound of Sugar, a spoonful of Rosewater a little sack a spoonful of Barm, & what spice you please. Beat it very well, then put into it one pound of clarified butter, one pound of flower & a pound of currans.

3 eggs	8oz 225g flour
1tsp 5ml rosewater	8oz 225g currants
8oz 225g sugar	1oz 25g fresh yeast or 7g sachet dried yeast
8oz 225g butter	1tsp 5ml mixed spice

If using fresh yeast, cream with a little of the sugar, then whisk the remaining sugar with the eggs. Melt the butter and add to the sugar and eggs with the remaining ingredients, including the dried yeast if using. Transfer to a lined 8inch 20cm cake tin and leave to rest for 30 minutes. Bake at Gas 4 350°F 180°C for approximately 40 minutes.

22. Robert May *The Accomplisht Cook*, London, 1685.

To make little Sugar Cakes

Take ye yolks of two eggs, & a quarter of a pound of sugar beaten very fine & mingle them well together then take half a pound of fresh butter & mix it well with ye sugar & eggs then take as much flower as will make it into a stiff past, & roll it out thin, cut them with a mold, bake them on thin plates, when they are brown in ye bottom they are enough.

2 egg yolks

4oz 100g sugar

8oz 225g butter, softened at room temperature

10oz 275g flour

Whisk the egg yolks and sugar together until light and creamy, then beat the butter into it. Add the flour gradually until it is all worked together. Roll out thinly and cut into rounds using a biscuit cutter. They hold their shape well so could if wished be cut into fancy shapes. Bake at Gas 4 350°F 180°C for approximately 12 minutes.

In spite of the name of these, they are not at all oversweet and make a delicious crisp biscuit.

To make small cakes

Take a pound of flower & so much butter, & one egg, four spoonfuls of ale yest some caraway seeds, put all together & make them in little cakes & shake suger on them you may bake them after bread.

1lb 450g flour

1lb 450g butter

1oz 2g fresh yeast or 7g sachet dried yeast

1 egg

1tsp 5ml caraway seeds

A little sugar

Cream fresh yeast with a teaspoon sugar, or add dried yeast to the flour, then beat all the ingredients together. Shape into small cakes and place on a greased baking tray. Sprinkle with sugar. Bake at Gas 4 350°F 180°C for around 15 minutes.

To make Queen Cakes

Take of flower, of Butter, of Currans & Sugar of each a pound, first mix your sugar & butter together with your hand in a pan half an hour, then putt in 6 eggs & take out 4 of ye whites, you must put in some spice & caraway seeds, then put in your flower & when your Oven is hott & your frames ready then put in your Currans & put them in your frames & strew some fine sugar on them.

8oz	225g	flour	8oz 225g	currants
8oz	225g	sugar	2tsp 10ml	ground ginger
8oz	225g	butter	1tsp 5ml	caraway seeds

Beat the butter and sugar together until light and fluffy, then beat in the eggs, stir in the flour and spices. This will give a thick paste, spread it in a swiss roll tin and bake in the centre of the oven at Gas 4 350°F 180°C for 20 – 25 minutes.

When I first tried this recipe I tried to cut them in rounds, but these do not hold their shape. Hence the instruction to cook them in frames. It does make an excellent tray bake, cut into squares to serve. I have omitted sprinkling sugar in the top as the recipe is already very sweet. Ginger works very well but you could use other spice instead.

A Garth Cake

Take half a peck of fine flower dry it well, 2 pounds of butter, a Pint of Cream, a Pint of Barm, rub ye Butter into ye flower wth 3 pounds of Currans one pound of Raisins stoned 3 Q^{rs} of a Pound of Sugar half an ounce of Nutmegs, Cloves and Mace each a qr of an ounce. One ounce of Limom & Orange peel 4 eggs a little sack & Rose water, mix it all together & cover it up close. Let it stand half an hour at the fire and so bake it.

12oz	350g	flour	2tbsp 30ml	sherry or brandy
4oz	100g	butter	1 egg	
5floz	75ml	cream	1tsp 5ml each cloves and nutmeg	
6oz	150g	currants	2tsp 10ml	rosewater
2oz	50g	raisins	1oz 25g	fresh yeast or 7 g sachet dried yeast
1½oz	40g	sugar		

Rub the butter into the flour, stir in the fruit, sugar, spice and dried yeast if using. Blend the fresh yeast with the cream and stir in the egg and wine. Mix into the dry ingredients. Put into a greased and lined 2 lb loaf tin and leave to rise for half an hour, no longer as it will continue to rise in the oven. Bake at Gas 5 375°F 190°C for approximately 30 minutes.

This is an eighth of the original quantity. The term 'Garth cake' suggests it should be cooked on a baking stone in the same way as the recipes below. Whilst having the advantage of missing out the lengthy process of heating the oven, it is hard to imagine cooking such a large quantity in this way.

Cake Mazerene

Take 2 p^d of fine flower a leven eggs white and all mix & beat y^m gently in ye flower then have redy on ye fire some butter & milk not to hot but pretty walme a quarter of a p^d of butter & half a point of milk will do when ye flower & egs are well mixt poure in y^r hot butter & milk but very softly, & stur it all ye time with y^r hand, put in some Brown Sugar a bout two or 3 spunfulls & a spunfull of good east & beat it well when it begins to bubble it is beat enough ye pan y^u intend to back it in must be butter'd & flowerd over it shuld be a tin pan with a cover it shuld be not quite half full when it is all in as it must have rome to rise then put it on some warme ashes & put some ashes on ye cover to make it rise & when it begins to rise very near ye top put it to ye oven but ye oven must not be to hot but y^u must take great care not to shake it as it will soon fall, to know when it is enough backed you must stick a knife into ye Middle & if it comes out clean it is enough then take it out of ye pan cut it in two or three as you would butter a hot role & pore in some melted butter & put some lofe sugar in y^r butter & some rose water & put some sweetmeats if you please to make it without an oven you have but to put ye ashes on all ye side & all about it yet not to hot & it will sone be don you have but to put your knife & try ye person who gaive me this Receite always makes it without an oven.

Cop^d

This recipe is written on the back of a letter, in a different hand and using different spelling conventions and showing a poorer command of written English than the other recipes. Interestingly, although it has been marked as 'copied' there is no copy of it in the handwritten booklets, which would imply that either someone other than the creator of this recipe collection has copied it out, and passed it onto the Gells afterwards, or there were at some point more recipes. Given that the recipe did not originate with the writer, it demonstrates the popularity, then, as now, of passing favourite recipes on.

1lb 450g flour	5floz 75ml milk
4 eggs	1oz fresh yeast or 7g sachet of dried yeast
2oz 50g butter	2oz 50g brown sugar

For filling: 1oz 25g butter and 1oz 25g sugar

If using dried yeast add it to the flour, make a well in the centre of the flour, and add the eggs, beaten. Warm the milk and butter together until the butter is just melted, and stir the fresh yeast into it. Beat it all well together and you will get something more akin to a batter than a dough. Transfer to a greased and lined 9 inch 23 cm round cake tin. Leave it to rise until it has doubled in size, then bake at Gas 5 375°F 190°C for approximately thirty minutes, until a skewer comes out clean from the centre of the cake. When it is cooked, melt the additional butter and blend with the sugar. Slice the cake horizontally whilst still hot and spread the mixture on the cake. If you like, you could add candied fruit, or dried fruit as well ('some sweetmeats if you please'), sandwich back together and leave to cool before serving.

To make Cakes Mrs A G

Rub 3 quar^{ts} of a pound of Butter into one pound of Flower, half a p^d of Sugar 2 eggs a large spoonful of white wine half a Nutmeg half an ounce of Carraways work it to a stiff paste, & put half a p^d of Currans.

12oz 350g butter		1tbsp 15ml white wine
1lb 450g flour		8oz 225g currants
8oz 225g sugar		2tsp 10ml nutmeg
2 eggs		2tsp 10ml caraway seeds

Stir the flour, spice and sugar together, rub the butter into it and then mix to a paste with the eggs and wine and stir the currants in. This will make a sticky mixture, if too sticky to handle, add a little extra flour. Use plenty of flour to roll out and cut into rounds. Place fairly well apart on baking trays and bake at Gas 4 350°F 180°C for 12 – 15 minutes, until a very pale gold.

To make excellent small cakes much esteemed at court

Take 3^{lb} of fine flower a pound & half of loaf sugar in fine powder 3^{lb} of currans, mix ye flower sugar & currans well together y^n put in a pound & half of unmelted butter 3 yolks of Eggs beat wth y^m one Nutmeg grated; when you wrought yor past well put it in a cloth & set it be fore ye fire till it be thro' warm then make y^ up in little cakes ye bigness of an hands breadth & prick y^ full of holes, & bake y^ in a quick oven unclosed.

1lb 450g flour		8oz 225g butter
8oz 225g sugar		1 egg
1lb 450g currants		1/3 nutmeg, grated

Stir the flour sugar currants and nutmeg together, and add the egg and butter and mix well to make a paste. If it is very stiff you may need to add a drop of milk. Shape into rounds and flatten. Prick them with the point of a knife and bake at Gas 6 400° F 200°C for 12 – 15 minutes.

To make Cakes

Take a pound of Flower, a pound of Butter & a pound of Sugar sifted, dry ye Flower & Sugar together & put in 2 parts, then take your pound of Butter & work it with your hand & shake in half your flower & Sugar keeping it beating with your hand, then take 8 eggs & half ye whites & 4 spoonfulls of Rose Water, then beat ye Eggs & warm ye Eggs & Rose water a little, then put in your sugar & flower with a dram of mace made fine keeping it still beating till all is in, then put in as many Carraway seeds as you please, then put them into tinn or Paper frames, & strew a little sifted sugar over them & so bake them.

8oz	225g	flour	1tsp	5ml	rosewater
8oz	225g	butter	1tsp	5ml	mace, ground
8oz	225g	sugar	1tsp	5ml	caraway seeds
4 egg yolks and 2 whites					

Mix the flour, sugar and mace together and beat the butter into half of it. Add the eggs and rosewater, and then gradually add the rest of the flour and sugar. Put into bun cases and bake at Gas 4 350°F 180°C for approximately 20 minutes.

To make Puff Cakes

Take a^{lb} of best flower a^{lb} of fresh butter wthout salt let ye butter lye all night in rosewater & A spoonfull of best barme a few caraway & coriander seeds wn they come out of ye oven Ice y^m or throw sugar on y^m prick well wn they goe into ye oven.

8oz	225g	flour	½oz fresh yeast or 7 g sachet dried yeast
8oz	225g	butter	1tsp 5ml rosewater

If using fresh yeast you will need to cream it with a little sugar to soften it. Mix all the ingredients together to make a dough and roll out and cut into rounds. If you omit sprinkling sugar on or icing them, they make a delicious rich crumbly biscuit to serve with cheese. For the sweetened version, either brush with milk and sprinkle with sugar, or apply a sugar glaze as they come out of the oven. Alternatively allow to cool and then apply a glace icing.

To make A good Cake

Lady Gower

Take 12 pound of the finest flower dry it very well then take 16 pound of Corinth clean washed and Picked they must be washed in several waters, the last water must be as warm as you can bear your hand in it, then drain them and dry them in a sheet or two, when so done set them by the fire to dry, then take A pound and halfe of good powdered Sugar A quarter of an ounce of Cloves & Mace A handful of salt two pound and halfe of Raisins of the Sun, Stoned and cut in Quarters, and dry them, then part your flower, put one halfe in ye tubb you design to make it in then strew your Cloves, Mace & salt into your flower, then take 3 pints of Cream 3 pound of butter, and your pound & halfe of Sugar which you dry'd, and almost A pint of Damask Rose water*, set these on ye fire and make them hot till ye butter be melted but let it not boyl take ye yolks of 36 Eggs and halfe of ye whites, very well beaten, then put to them 3 pints of ye best ale yeast, beat the yeast & Eggs very well together then strain them into your flower, as also your Cream and butter and Rosewater and sugar mix all these together till all ye Lumps are broken, then bake ye rest of your flower and strew it all over and cover it with A Linnen Cloth, and A Blankett four times doubled, set it before ye fire till the flower begins to crack on ye top, then take it and work it well and put in your Raisins & Currans and mix all well together for a Quarter of an hour, put in two pound of almonds beat & shred, and set it to ye fire to rise again till your Oven is ready, then make ready your hoop & cut papers fit for your hoop butter & stick them close to your hoop on ye inside with past, when your oven is ready put your cake into your hoop and set into the oven, if it colour too much lay a sheet of paper on the top, so let it stand at least 3 hours before you ice it then take A pound & halfe of double refined sugar beat and searched mix it with a little Rose water & ye white of an Egg beaten to A froth, Let not your icing be too thick when you put it on your cake, set it in ye Oven to dry.

Add 3 pound of Orange Lemmon pill & Cittern.

*half brandy dooth best

An Excellent Seed Cake

Take 2 pound of Butter & melt it in a saucepan, then pouer it into an earthernpott, the next day, scrape it clean from ye butter milk, Rubb it very well into a quarter of a peck of flower dryed in ye Oven, knead it with 9 Eggs beaten with a pint of Sack, & Rose water together then sett before ye fire that it may rise whilst ye Oven is heating hot enough for Manchett then work in 2 pounds of Carroway Confitts & then put it in your frame it will be baked in less than an hour.

4.5 Preserves and Banqueting Stuff

Preserving fruit was a vitally important part of the role of a housewife, and there were many ways to do this. Many of the preserves would have been served as they were, as part of the banquet course. Some would have been preserved to use in fruit pies and tarts, making them more of a jam tart as we would understand them. Fruits could also be preserved in syrup.

Lemon, orange, apricot, quince, apple, pippin, gooseberry, codling, plum, cherry, malligotoon, pear, warden, raspberry and redcurrant were all preserved in some form. Warden was a winter pear, codling and pippin were apples. A variety of fruit which proved elusive to identify, the malligotoon is an alternative spelling for the mellacatton, and the recipe is similar to the two identical recipes found in Robert May and William Rabisha's works.[14] The mellacatton is variously described as a variety of peach, or as a peach grafted onto a quince. This would have made it a hardier tree, and therefore presumably easier to grow in the English climate. Strawberries are not mentioned, although they were available at that time, perhaps because they are not much used in a cooked form. There is a recipe for preserving peach flowers, although not for peaches themselves. We do know that Elizabeth Gell at Hopton Hall was sent a gift of conies and peaches in 1614 from Bridget Wyllughbye at Wollaton Hall, Nottingham, so we know that it was possible to grow them in this area. However, the fact that they were a gift may indicate that they were a speciality.

The term marmalatt or marmalade referred in the seventeenth century to an earlier version which was a very stiff paste. This was served with other preserved fruits as part of the banquet course. Over time it became less solid and was used as a spread. It was because its medicinal properties were thought to be more effective on an empty stomach that it became part of breakfast. Anne Wilson has written an excellent book on this topic if you wish to pursue it further.[25] The usual fruit at this time was not orange, but quince, though the recipe for 'Welch Marmalade' uses damson.

The alternative method of preserving fruit was to candy it, this involves a combination of boiling the fruit in a sugar syrup, and then drying it either in the sun or in an oven. These could have been used in cakes, as we still use candied peel, or served as dessert. It is a time consuming process, involving much boiling up, cooling, re-boiling and laying out to dry. Simply preparing the large quantities of fruit used would have taken a lot of time. To dry plums is a process that takes four to five days, including wiping each plum individually, and stuffing them, the stone having been previously removed, with a very thick paste 'meat' made from plums for that purpose. It would have been hot work.

Some of the recipes that appear initially to be cakes, are in fact fruit preserves either dropped on to papers or tins and baked, or poured onto plates and baked. A lot is made of the need to soak oranges to remove the bitterness, indicating that the oranges available would have been the bitter Seville oranges, still preferred for making marmalade today.

24. Rabisha, William *The whole body of cookery dissected...*, London 1682
25. Wilson, C. Anne *The book of marmalade*, Prospect Books, 1999

Sugar, used in large quantities here, was relatively expensive, but readily available, and the nature of the recipes do show the relative affluence of the household. Honey is not used as a sweetener or preservative in any of the food recipes. Sugar was purchased in loaves, and depending on the price was either refined once or twice. Many recipes specify double refined sugar, or the recipe includes instructions on clarifying the sugar. Sugar became much cheaper during the early part of the Eighteenth century.

There are no recipes for marchpane[26], perhaps it was one of those classic recipes that need not be written down, or perhaps it was not used as much as published cookery books would imply, as it does not appear on the menu plans in the collection either.

Unless you wish to make something comparable to the eighteenth century preserves, and if you would like to be able to spread these preserves on bread, I would suggest boiling the marmalades until a setting point is reached, as generally accepted in making preserves and jams.

To preserve ripe Apricocks

Gather yr Apricocks of a fine Colour, but not too ripe; weigh them, & to every pound of cocks put a p^d of Double refined Sugar beaten & sifted; Stone & pare y^r Apricocks; & as y^u pare 'em put 'em into ye pan, wth Sugar Strew'd over & under them, let 'em not touch one another, cover em up & let em ly till ye next Day, then stir them gently till ye Sugar is melted, then put them on a quick fire & let em boil half an hour, skimming exceeding well all ye while then take 'em off & cover em till ye next Day then boil em again, skimming 'em very well till tis enough, so put em in pots.

1lb 450g apricots

1lb 450g sugar

Stone the apricots and if you are patient enough you may peel them although I did not. Layer them with the sugar in a bowl or pan, and leave overnight. In the morning the sugar will have turned to syrup. Boil them for half an hour, and then leave to cool.

To make Quince Marmaylett

Take a pound of Sugar beaten & put as much water to it as will something more than wett it, then sett it in y' fire & Scumm it, then take a pound of Quinces when they are cored & paired & put them in your sirrup & let them boyl very leasurely being covered, then take a quart of water & put into it your cores & pairings & let them boyl till it be very strong, then strain out almost half a pint of that water & put to your Quinces & let them boyl leasurely till they are tender & look a good colour then take them up out of y' sirrup & beat them small with a spoon in a Porringer & when it is small enough, put it into your sirrup again & boyl it a little longer & so glaze it up; your Quinces must boyl but a very little while in y' sirrup before your water that boyled the cores in.

1lb 450g sugar	8floz 240ml water
1lb 450g quince	2 pints 1200ml water

Dissolve the sugar in the 8floz of water and bring to the boil. Add the quartered quinces and cover the pan and simmer. Meanwhile, put the peel and cores in a pan and cover well with 2 pints of water. Bring to the boil and keep boiling. Strain this and add half a pint of this water to the quinces. When the quince are tender take them out and beat or liquidise them, and then return them to the syrup and boil until a setting point is reached. Pot as for jam.

Quinces when boiled turn a lovely deep red colour, which is what this recipe refers to. This makes a very pleasant alternative to Quince jelly, which is the usual recipe made with quince. These are English quince, rather than the ornamental Japanese quince.

To make Marmalett of Oranges

Take your oranges & pare them as thin as possibly you can then cut them in the middle & squeeze out y' juice & put it into anything & cover it till you have occasion to use it then lay your Oranjes in water 3 days then boyl them & shift till bitterness be out of them, then take a pint of pippin water & a pound of y' best loaf sugar & let it boyl in your pan till it is candy High then put your orange in & half a pound of it being cut in square bits & as much of your juice of Orange & Lemon as please your palate & let it boyl a little & then take it off y' fire & let it stand a little & put it into your glasses for use.

2lb 900g oranges	1lb 450g sugar
1pt 600ml apple juice	

Using a potato peeler, peel the oranges and soak the peel in water overnight. Simmer the peel in water for 30 minutes, until it is tender, and cut into short pieces. Boil the sugar, apple juice and the juice of the oranges together until setting point is reached, or for a more authentic consistency contine boiling for approximately ten minutes longer. Stir the peel in and transfer to warmed jars. Pot and cover as for jam.

To p^{rserve} ye Pippin, Pear or warden dry

First take the clearest pippins you can get pare y̅ & core y̅ very clean either in halfes or whole yⁿ take so much fair water as will suffice to make y̅ & set it on ye fire untill they be ready to boyl so done put in your fruit & let it boyl a little space yⁿ take y̅ off from ye fire, & let y̅ stand close covered, till they be very soft yⁿ when you feel y^m soft take y̅ out of ye hot liquer & put y̅ in cold & let y̅ lye for half an hour yⁿ take y̅ out, & let y̅ lye two or 3 hours upon a searce to dry so done take for ye weight of y^{or} fruit so much sugar or more & wth a quantity of rosewater dissolve yor sugar to one pound half a pint of rosewater wth a little fair water, & wth ye white of an egg, clarify yor sugar & strain it, so done, set it over ye fire again, & let it boil untill it be come to a p^{fect} height, which is when it will a little cleave between yor fingers & thumb, then presently put in your fruit & let it boyl a little space then take it off & let it stand half a quarter of an hour, yⁿ set it on ye fire again, & let y̅ boyl till such time as you find yor syrrup so thick y^t it will roap betwixt yor fingers, then take y̅ from ye fire, & let y̅ stand as long as before then take y̅ forth, & lay y̅ one be one upon a searce to drip ye space of two hours, setting a thing under it to receive ye syrrup, so lay y̅ on boards to dry.

To make Walnut Catchup

Take a Hundred of walnuts when fit to pickle let them be laid in salt & water for two days let them be shifted twice in the time, then take them out & beat them in a marble mortar however not brass, then put them in an Earthen pot with a Pint of Vinegar & an handful of salt & let them be stirred every day then strain it very hard then boyl it half a quarter of an hour, of mace a quarter of an ounce a few cloves a quantity of black pepper a little race of ginger an anchovy or two & let it boyl a quarter of an hour, it must not be boyled in brass when it is cold bottle it up with the spices in it, cork it up well & tie a piece of leather over it. Put the Pig²⁷ into it so keep it for Use.

To pickle Cucumers, Elderbuds, broombuds, Ashkeys, purslain stalks &c.

Gather y̅ on a dry day yⁿ take 3 quarts of water & 4 quarts of white wine vinegar 3 handfull of salt a handfull of dill 24 bay leaves one ounce of whole pepper, as much whole ginger set ye over ye fire & put in a piece of allom & let it boyle well & put in ye things you intend into an earthern pot & put ye pickle to y̅ scalding hot & cover down close wth a piece of leather 3 daies after uncover y^m & put in 2 or 3 spoonfull of sweet oyle & y^t will preserve y̅ wth Mother all ye year keeping y^m close covered in a cold place for yor use.

27. In this context, a stopper.

To make Indian Pickle

Put one pound of Ginger into salt & water, let it lye one Day & Night, then cut it in slices & put it into a mug with Dry Salt till the other ingredients are ready. Viz one pound of Garlick, peel it & cut it in peices – lay it in salt & water Three Days. Wash it and let it lye in Dry Salt three Days longer, then wash it again & lay it in the Sun or near the Fire to dry – a Quarter of a pound of white mustard seed & one ounce of Turmerick; Bruise the two latter in a mortar together; put all these into a bout four or five Quarts of Vinegar & give them a boil up when the pickle is ready, Cabbage Collyflower, Radish & Sallery must be salted with Dry salt three Days then dryed by Sun or Fire, French beans must only lye in salt 2 Days Cucumber melons peaches Apples Carrats are to lye in salt 3 days, all these things may be put in the a bove pickle together & will keep for years, only adding fresh vinegar, & salting & Drying whatever you put in the a bove manner.

NB mangos to be put in the same pickle fill them with mustard seed & little garlick & hore radish.

A simplified version of this recipe was tried, and whilst salty worked very well when served with a contemporary gammon pie as a pickle.

To preserve Malligotoons[28]

Take Malligotoons & boyle y^m tender in fair water & let y^m stand still till they be cold then pare & pick y^m with a knife to ye stone then put y^m into as much clarified sugar as will cover them, so let y^m boyl leisurely 3 or 4 hours you need not fear breaking y^m for they will boyl like a piece of beef when they be boyled tender take y^m up & boyling ye syrrup a little by it self, then betwixt hot and cold you may put y^m up, & keep y^m all ye year.

28. A variety of peach. This recipe is taken from Rabisha (ibid).

4.6 Ale, Wine and such like

The place where honey comes into its own is in the making of mead. There are eight mead recipes included in the collection, indicating both its popularity and the availability of large quantities of honey. With four pounds of honey to each gallon of water a considerable amount would have been used. Mead was flavoured with a variety of herbs or spices and was regarded as being beneficial to health. The water and honey would be boiled together until a certain specific gravity was reached, being shown by the ability of the boiling liquid to support the weight of an egg, so that a certain amount of the shell showed above the surface. The recipe for Metheglin, a spiced version of mead, gives instructions on how to do this.

There are 59 wine recipes in the collection, more than a tenth of the recipes altogether. The most popular types are cowslip, raisin and elderberry. Several have been included as examples, although a modern version has not been given as very few people make their own wine these days. There is a group of wine recipes taken from Hartman's 'Family Physitian'[29] and attributed as such.

Whilst there are no recipes for ale or beer included, because it was such a vital part of the household's production it can safely be assumed that ale was being produced in large quantities as the standard drink for everyone.

To make a sack Posset

Take 24 eggs & beat y̅ very well with all y̅ᵉ whites, & set y̅ over y̅ᵉ fire w̅ᵗʰ a pint of sack, a pound of double refined sugar & one nutmeg sliced, stirr it continually one way, & let it stand till it be as hot as you can abide your finger in it y̅ put to it 2 quarts of boyling hot milk y̅ⁿ take it from y̅ᵉ fire & cover it with a hott plate & set it between two cushions & let it stand half an hour, then strew some Cinnument & sugar over it. You may put in some perfume plumbs if you please.

6 eggs

4floz 120ml white wine

3oz 90g sugar

1pt 600ml milk

1tsp 5ml nutmeg, grated

Heat most of the milk gently with the nutmeg, leaving a little aside to stir into the eggs. Stir the cold milk into the beaten eggs and add to the warm milk, stirring and heating gently. Heat the wine separately, and when it is warm pour the milk into it, ideally from a height to make it froth. Sprinkle with a little more sugar and cinnamon, and let it stand a short while in a warm place and it will thicken somewhat.

Recipes in published cookery books of the period usually use cream rather than milk, and I have adjusted the method of this a little to reflect these. Anything from eight to 24 eggs, sometimes just the yolks, are used to this quantity of cream, which seems to be the usual amount made at one time.

29. Hartman, George *The Family Physitian*, London, 1696

To make a Sack Posset

Take 2 quarts of good cream a quarter of a^{lb} of almonds, stamp y^e & put y^e in y^e cream & boyl it & take a pint of sack in a Bason & set it on a chafingdish till it be blood warme then take y^e yolks of 12 eggs with 4 whites & beat y$^-$ very well & put y$^-$ in y^e sack then stirr all together over y^e coals till it be as thick as you would have it. You may grind some musk & Ambergrise & Sugar & strew over it to make it pleasant.

Whilst the wording is a little different, this recipe is identical to one of several in The Accomplisht Cook.[30] Some of the other recipes use grated biscuit to thicken, rather than almonds.

To make Imperiall

Take 6 quarts of Water, 2 ounce of Cream of Tartar, ye Peel of 2 Lemons. Boyl these together a little while, & sweeten it with Loaf Sugar to y^r taste.

3 pts 1800ml water		Peel of 1 lemon
¼ oz 7g Cream of tartar		Sugar to taste

Simmer the water, cream of tartar and lemon peel together for 30 minutes. Take out the peel, stir in sugar to taste and then pour into a jug to cool.

This makes a refreshing tangy drink, with a hint of sherbet.

Mrs Mauds receipt to make Elder Wine

Take 3 gallons & a ½ of water, sett it over ye fire when it is warm put into it a peck of Elderberrys, bruife then very well in it, then straine y^m out then meafure how many quarts you have of this Liquor & to every quarts put a p^d of honey boy it together till it will bear an egg, keep scumming it all the while then take it off the fire, Let it stand till it be as cold as ale when you put on ye yest, then, to every 2 quartes put a pint of new ale that is working. Let all work together a day & a night, then tun it into a rundlet. When it hath done working, stop it up clofe, & Let it stand till Christmas before you breach it, if you pleafe you may boyle this will keep a year.

30. Robert May *The Accomplisht Cook,* London, 1685 (Facsimilie edition, Prospect Books, 2000

Untitled Raisin wine recipe

April y 13 1750 we put together a hundred of Smyrna black raisins & sixteen gallons & a half o' water, Ale measure, unboiled, it stood in the tub 3 weeks & was stirr'd every Day then the raisins were squeezed out by handfuls & the liquor was out into a Barrel, the Barrel was almost full, it stood in the Barrell about two months & was then rack'd off and put into the Barrell again with an ounce of Isinglass dissolved in some of it. The Barrel was not washed but rubbed with a cloth, it stood till was quite clear and then we Bottled it on St Jame's Day 25ᵗʰ July.

The right method of making Metheglin

Having made yᵒʳ water blood warme in yᵒʳ copper or kittle put yᵉ hony to it about one part to 4 of water but because yˢ doth not determine yᵉ proportions exactly (for some hony will make it stronger yⁿ other) you must do yᵗ by bearing up an Egg ; but first lade & scoop yᵒʳ mixture exceedingly (at least an hour) yᵗ yᵉ hony be not perfectly dissolved but uniformly mixᵗ throughout yᵒʳ water then take out some of it in a great wooden bowl or pail & put a good number 10 or 12 newlaid Eggs into it & as round ones as may be for long ones may deceive you in yᵉ swimming & stale ones being lighter yⁿ new will emerge out of yᵉ waterye breadth of a 6 pence wⁿ new ones will not a groat breadth, therefore you take many yᵗ you may make a medium of their several Emergins, unless you be certain ȳ those wᶜʰ you use are immoderately yⁿ laid & very round yᵒʳ rule is thᵗ a groat or rather a 3 pence breadth of yᵒʳ egg shell must swim above yᵉ liquor wᶜʰ put again into yᵒʳ copper to boyl so soon as it boyls turn up an hourglass & let it boyl gently an hour a quarter before yᵉ hour is out put into it some Eringo roots sliced small & a little ginger in fine powder & a sprig of dry rosmary wᶜʰ having boyled a quarter of an hour to make up yᵉ whole hour of boyling pour out yᵉ liquor into wide open fat to coole. When it is quite cold tunn it up into a Cask yᵗ has had Sack in it or white port wine; let it forment of it self without yest keeping a thick plate of lead upon yᵉ bung to lay close upon it so yᵗ yᵉ working of yᵉ liquor may raise it to purge of yᵉ foulness, & have alwaies some new made plain liquor to fill it up as it sinks. Wⁿ it has done working left huzzing & is quiet yⁿ stop yᵉ bung exceedingly close & let it ly 3 or 4 months alwaies keeping yᵉ Cask full & wⁿ you begin to draw it bottle it. It will become a more pleasant vinous drink daily loosing³¹ its luscious tast: yᵉ longer it is kept yᵉ better it will be wⁿ you barrel it up. Hang in it a bag to yᵉ proportion of 15 gallons an ounce of cinnamon clove & mace of each an ounce all grossly beaten for if you beat it fine it will alwaies float in yᵒʳ Metheglin & make it foul & if you put it in whilst it is hot yᵉ spices will loose their spirits. In yᵉ boyling it do not skum it for yᵗ afterwards promotes fermentation more natural yⁿ wᵗʰ yeast & more holdsome yn otherwaies for if you make it work wth yeast you must have a great care to draw it into bottle soon after it hath done working or after a fourtnight or 3 weeks for yᵗ will make it soon grow stale & it will thence grow sour & dead before you are aware but if it work of it self singly wthout leven or yeast it may be kept long in yᵉ barrel so it be fill'd up to yᵉ top & kept very close stopt.

31. releasing

To make Cock Ale

Dress a Red Cock, parboyl him a quarter of an hour, pull off his skin & bruise him well in a Mortar, put to him a quart of Canary, when he has been steeped 24 hours put him & ye Liquour into six Gallons of ale, as soon as it has done working take one pound of Razons of ye Sun, Stoned, & two ounces of Dates sliced 2 Nutmegs & a few cloves & some mace stop it up close & at ten days old bottle it.

To Make Cowslip Wine

To every Gallon of Water take 2 pd of Powder Sugar let it boyl an hour, then scumm it clean & strain it as you do Wort, & when it is cold enough put a little yest into it, & when it hath gathered a White head put it into your Vefsel, & put into it 5 quarts of Cowslips picked, put in ye juice of 2 or 3 Lemons, & ye Peel of one, stir it well together & stop ye Vefsel close & let it stand 3 or 4 Weeks, then bottle it. If ye Whether be coole, let it stand longer, be sure lett your Vessel be too big by 2 or 3 Gallons else ut will work over & make mad work.

To Make Goosberry Vinegar

To every Gallon of Cold Water put six pound of ripe Gooseberrys Bruised in Mortar with a Wooden pestil, put them into a clean vefsel, then pour y^r water upon them, & stir them up, set' em in a warm place near a Kitchen fire or in the Sun till the liquor ferments, & ye Fruit rise to ye Top, which will be about a fortnight. Then draw off ye Liquor & strain ye Berries from it, Clean it & strain ye Liquor into ye same Cask, to every Gallon of it put one pound of Brown Sugar, which will make it Ferment a second time, when ye see it has done working, stop it close, it will be fit for use in about 6 months, it must be kept in a warm place which will add to its goodness, & ripen it ye sooner, Cristall gooseberries are ye best, but any will do for common use. Be sure use none for pickles, but w^t is made Cristall gooseberries.

To make Mead

Boil yor water an Hour, to every gallⁿ of which put four lbs of Honey, mix y^m well together & boil it two Hours more, keeping it clean scum'd, & when it is cold put it into yor vefsel, bung it close, & let it stand half a year or a year before you bottle it.

If you have a large stock of Honey it is an excellent method of using it, for the above rec^t makes a charming wine, if kept to be old.

To make Reason Wine

Take half a hundred of Raisins of y Sun and let y great stalks be pick out, then chop them in a tub and put to them ten Gallons of Water That has boyled an hour, when it is all most Cold cover it and let it stand till it works of it self Stiring it once a day till then, and when it Does work you must ftir y Raisins down when it has workd fore or five days then strayn them out and press them in a press if you have not one you must wring them very dry in Som course then put y Liquor in a Barrell that will hold a gallon more than you put in, and let it Stand 6 months be fore you peg it, and take care it is not Shook for it is hard to Settle again, when it is fine bottle it, and it will keep some years.

Mrs Wrights rec for Raisin Wine

Six pounds of Raisins to one Gallon of Water Wine measure. To stand together ten Days.

12. Recipe to cure worms in children (NA DD/E/59/57/39)   13. Heart shape the plaster should be spread on (NA DD/E/59/57/34)

4.7 Cures and domestic

As well as the collection of recipes for dying cloth and for perfumes for different items, predominantly gloves, which are copied into the back of Thomas Gell's recipe collection, there are scattered amongst the rest of the recipes a variety of recipes for curing varying ailments, of both people and horses, as well as those for varying domestic purposes. Whilst there are no recipes for it, it is likely that rosewater would have been distilled at home. **I am including a selection of these recipes for interest and completeness, but must emphasise that these should not be used.** I have to admit that, interesting although these are, I have not tried them!

A Milk Snail Water

Take a gallon of new milk, put a soo of shell snails washed & cracked, throw away yᵉ loose shells, take a pint of earthworms clean washed & slit, boyl them all in yᵉ milk half an hour, then put to it harts=tongue, Alehoofe, Cowslips of Jerusalem, Pimpernell, Coltsfoot of each an handful, spearmint two handful, cut them to lye in the still with a pretty hot fire & stir it often, let it drop on sugar candy, 2 ounces to a quart & give six or seven spoonful in a day.

There is no indication given as to what this was meant to cure, I'm sure it was very effective.

For a Soar Throat

Take a handful of Cotton Weed boil it verry slowly or simmer it in a pint of milk till half is consumed then strain it off and gargle the throat with verry often in the day, it must be warm when used.

NB If any is swallowed there is not the least Danger.

To make a Plaister for the Worms in Children

Take two Penniworth of Chimicall Oil of Wormwood, and two penniworth of Methridate[32] spread upon sheep skin. Mix your oil and methridate together and then spread it, anoint the stomacke with some Chimmical Oil of Wormwood before you lay the plaster on the plaster must be in the Form of a Heart it must be swathed on and a string taked to the little end, and hanged about the Neck [observe the form of the plaster on the other leaf]

in the forme of this bit of paper

My wife would have made the plaister but it could not be carried after it was spread.

This recipe was obviously inserted into a letter, and then copied out. There is a cut out piece of paper to indicate exactly what shape to make this poultice.

---

32. Mithridate: A composition of many ingredients in the form of an electuary, regarded as a universal antidote or preservative against poison & infectious disease. Hence any medicine to which similar powers were ascribed (OED).

To make Hungary Water

The best way to make it is of spirits of Wine or of spirits of your stilling if not of brandy as you get your rosemary flowers put them into your spirits to infuse & stop them close put in till your spirits will just cover them then still them off & when stilled then put in flowers as before & still them again & so do till you have stilled them 3 times if you make your own spirits you must still the spirits 3 times before you begin to make the water & 3 times when the flowers are in you must put in lavender flowers which mends it.

For ye Toothach

Take pepper & grains of each an ounce bruise y⁻ & compound wth yᵉ water³³ of yᵉ diseased & make it of a good thickness & lay it outward on yᵉ cheek against yᵉ place & it will help it.

A Receipt for a strain in the Back Sinews of a Horse

One Quart of old Crab Verjuice one Pint of Spring Water One Handfull of Common Salt ¼th of Pound of bol Armeniack Boiled together and Bath the part well, then dip in a Hay Band in the Liquor and bind it round the part strained, you may power some of yᵉ Liquor upon yᵉ Band after it is fixed upon his Leg, if there is any that the Band did not drink up.

A Receipt for a Sprain

Half a pint of the Best Goosberry Vinegar one ounce of Salt Petre sifted to a very fine powder Two Table Spoonfulls of Spirits of Turpentine. Mix them well in a Bottle tile the Saltpetre is Disolved then apply to the part strained Rubing it with a warm Hand before the Fire and if a bad strain bind it afterwards with Flannel.

If this be well corked in Bottles it will keep for years.

To make Aqua Mirablis

Take sack 3 Quarts, Cloves, Mace, Nutmegs & Ginger of each two drams; a pint of yᵉ juice of Bawme, as much juice of mint, a quart of yᵉ juice of Celandine, 3 pints of Cowslips & a handfull off Borage flowers, a quart of red rose water & a quart of strong angelica water & so mix all these together in an earthern pott & lett it stand all night & yᵉ next morning put it in your still with a handfull of Herts tongue in yᵉ bottom of your still yⁿ do yᵉ edges of your still wᵗʰ past.

Putting pastry around the edge of the still would have provided a seal in the same way as it could be used on an oven door.

33. Water in this case means urine. This was used both in some cures and for diagnosis of conditions.

61

To get Ink Stains out of Linnen

Take Sope & fine Salt & rub it on ye Stains dry & wash it out wth boyling Vinegar.

To make Plague Water

Take Rosemary. Sage, Celandine, Mugwort, Wormwood, Pimpernel, Scordium, Cardums, maidenhaire, Hartstongue, Agrimony, rhue, Liverwort, marjerom, Centaury, Marygolds, Bettony, borrage, green wallnuts, Angelica, Woodsorrel of each a handfull, roots of elicampe, Tormentill, Cypruss, Gentian of each half an ounce. Let ye herbs be bruised & ye roots sliced & infused in 10 q^{rts} of common spirits for 12 hours y^n let y̅ be distilled wth a slow fire according to art.

A Receipt for the Rhumatism

1 pennyworth of winters Bark Broke into Small bitts some Horse Reddish slised a handful of Scurvy Grass Leavs an up heaped spoonfull of Mustard Seed Grosly Brused put all these togeather into a bottle that will hold 3 pints fill it up with white wine & when it has stood 12 hours it is fitt for use. Drink a wine Glass of it in ye Morning an Hour before you rise & att Night going to bed be sure to keep warm it frequently occations sweating: NB when ye bottle is half Emty it will bear filling up again.

Syrrup of Buckthorne

Make a strong decoction of Sena to an ounce of sena half a dram of salt of tartar add some juniper berries & ginger to correct or coriander seeds then take ye decoction & pour it upon ye Buckthorne berries y^n squeese y̅ almost to a muscilage wth y^{or} hands let y̅ stand 24 hours to ferment heat y̅ till they gently boyl y^n strain y̅ in a press hard y^n let ye juice settle till it be clear pour of ye clear & in every pint of y^{or} liqr dissolve 2lb & 4 ounces of sugar strain it again through a coarse napkin y^n bottle it close w^n it is cold.

To make Lavender Drops

Take a quart of Lavender flowers steep them a week in 3 pints of Spirrits of Whine strain it through a fine flannel add to It a small handful of Orange leaves Cut Small one ounce of Piony Seeds Cloves Cinamon Nutmegs Cardimums of Each a quarter of an ounce and one Dram of Saffron Let it stand a fortnight Close Stopt then pour off the Clear Liequor for use.

Balls for ye Quare of Surfit in Horses

Take Castille soap 12 ounces, Salopunnell, Suggie Candy, yellow Kofen, Cled Brimstone, of each three ounces, Balsom of Sulphur one ownce, Ciratene of Antimony ½ oz, A sufficient quantity of Honey to mix it into Balls, when all yͤ ingredients are reduced small to mix wth honey near as hard as yͤ Castle soap – Give yͤ Horses two Balls for a dose about as large as a Hen Egg Each – This may be given either in a morning or after exercise requiring to be led an Hour before and half an hour after it – Give him warm water the same day – And repeat these Balls once in 3 or 4 for 2 or 3 doses And of certain requirith once a fortnight or 3 weeks.

These Balls take off Greasy Swelling and clenses Horses from foul Humours, gets and makes a fine skin. If you have been Hunting you may give yͤ Horse yͤ two Balls, as you come home taking care that he doth not go into water.

May yͤ 2ⁿᵈ 1750

To Glaze Callico

Take 3 pints of fair water & 3 oz of white starch and with it make a fine thin clear starch water, & when well boyled have ready 4 oz of fine white wax shaved very fine & put it into a pot then take the starch boyling hot & straine it to yͤ wax & keep it till the wax be all dissolved then take a spune & wet the Callico all over with yͤ starch you must keep your so warm that the wax may not be cold first you must wash the Callico very clean & Rense it with blew water & clap it down very smooth, When it is bone dry you must put pluck it out very well then do it with the spunge & starch upon a clean Board, & when it is so done hang it up very smooth till it is better than half dry. Then iron it upon a clean dry board without a cloth till your Callico be dry, it will look Glazed very well but you must take what care you can you do not shake off the wax that will lye upon the Callico.

An infallible cure for a Sore throat

A quarter of a pound of mutton suit taken from the Kidnies three ounces of fresh butter four ounces of Rosin powdered one ounce an half of Bees Wax sliced melt ye Mutton Suit strain it then put it to ye Butter when melted over a gentle fire add to it the Rosin & Bees Wax keep it stiring over the fire till melted then put it into gallipots stiring it till near Cold it will keep good a year or two when you use it Spread it cold on a linen cloth three or fore inches broad. Put it on from ear to ear putting a piece of flannel over it afresh plaister in twenty four hours if wanted but one generally does if taken in time it often occasions a Rash where yͤ plaister was when you take off the plaister put on a Flannel for a day or two for fear of Cold.

For a cold

Take four Handfulls of Gill to a quart of Spring water, Boyl it a way to a pint, then strain it off, and put half a pound of Brown Sugar Candy, and Boyl it to a Surrop.

To make Green Salve

Take half a pound of sheeps suet being first clarified, & a pound of Rauzen, & half a pound of Bees wax, & 2 pennyworth of Verdigrase made into powder put all these into a Posnett, & sett it over a gentle fire & let it boyl 2 or 3 walms, then take it off & stir into it half a pennyworth of Turpentine & then pour it out & work it well with your hands & make it up in Rolls & so keep it in a box, it is good for Burns & all manner of old sores & green wounds.

A Diett Drink for ye Dropsie

Take Water Cressettes & Brook lime of each 2 handfulls sharp Dock Roots half a pound, roots of Dwarf Elder one pound, broome Ashes a pint Juniper Berryes two ounce let yᵉ roots be slit, & yᵉ herbs cutt, & yᵉ Berryes bruised, & put them all in a bag, & hang the Bag in yᵉ Vefsell to 3 or 4 gallons of small ale, when it hath done working & when it is a week old drink a quarter of a pint in yᵉ morning fasting & yᵉ like an hour & half before Dinner & at 4 in yᵉ Afternoon.

The directions for taking this medicine suggest that dinner was taken around midday.

To perfume gloves

First wash yoʳ leather in cold water 3 or 4 times yⁿ steep it in rosewater a while & after crush out yᵉ water & hang it up till it be almost dry but still rubb it or stretch it to keep it from going hard yⁿ hang it over a chafing dish of coals wᵗʰ a cover lid to keep in yᵉ smoak putting in sweet past eight or nine times under yⁿ wrap it up in some piece of silk close to keep it from yᵉ Air where it must lye one whole day & a night & yⁿ wⁿ you have rubbed & smoothed yᵐ they are ready for yᵉ perfume. Then take Gum dragon & lay it one whole night to steep in rosewater yⁿ put yoʳ Musk into a mortar & having beaten it a little take so much gum & rosewater as will make it into a syrrup or of half an ounce of musk make almost a pint yⁿ empty yᵉ mortar & heat it hot & put in your amber & of oyl of Jessamine yⁿ put in yor Civet & stirr it well together wᵗʰ yᵉ juice of half a Lemon & two little pieces of yᵉ pill yⁿ put in yᵉ musk again & set it on yᵉ fire still stirring it, & when tis hot work it into yᵉ Leather.

King Henry's Perfume

Take a q^{rter} of an ounce of Fussis & twopenny weight of good cloves & let y^m be a little bruised y^n take one pennyweight of ye rind of a lemon in powder & six spoonfull of damask rosewater & A spoonfull of fair clean water & let all these boyl together in a p^{fume} pann wth ye quantity of a hazel nut of sugar.

All manner of herbs good for Perfumes

Sweet basil dried in Summer cut small & kept in baggs wth violets ye green being cut off then take ye buds of red roses ye whites being cut off — these 3 being mingled together wth sugar & rosewater do make an excellent p^{fume}. Bay leaves green are good tempered wth rose water & vinegar for ye head & ye leaves of walnuts being young wth rosewater & young red mints are very good dried.

April ye 13, 1750 we put together a hundred of Smyrna Raisins, & Sixteen Gallons, & a halfe water, Alemeasure, unboild, it stood in the Tub 3 weeks & was stirr'd every Day, then the raisins were squeez'd out by handfull, & the liquor was put into a Barrel, the Barrel was almost full. it stood in the Barrell about two months & was then rack'd off and put into the Barrell again, with an ounce of Iceinglass dissolved in some of it. the Barrell was not wash'd but rub'd with a cloth, it stood till 'twas quite clear and then we Bottl'd it. on Sr James's Day, 25 of July.

To make a Seed cake
Take one pound of Flower, one pound of Butter, one p^d. Sugar 12 Eggs leaving out 6 of the whites one ounce of carraway seeds y^u must beat the Butter till it almost as thin as cream before y^u put in the above things and y^u must beat it an hour after, a little Rosewater, or good wine wou'd do good, it will make good Queen cakes adding a pound of currans.

14. Details of wine making from 1750 (NA DD/E/59/56)

5. Weights and Measures

Weights

lb. =   16 oz.

st. =   14 lb., except = 8 lb (almonds, cumin, pepper, sugar, wax, and beef in London)

qr. (quarter) = 2 st. = 28 lb.

Measures

qt. (quart)	=	2 pt (pint)
gallon	=	4 quarts
p (peck)	=	2 gallons
bu (bushel)	=	4 pecks
	=	8 gallons
	=	32 quarts.
qr (quarter)	=	8 bushels
Pot	=	1 quart
Tankard	=	1 quart
Pottle	=	2 quarts
Strike	=	2 bushels
Hogshead	=	54 gallons
Pipe	=	2 hogsheads
Rundlett	=	18 gallons

6. Glossary

Ambergrise	Aromatic resin secreted by whales
Bacon natch	Something from which to hang bacon
Chaffing dish	A dish for holding charcoal or warm coals to provide a gentle heat to cook over.
Chocolate mill	A whisk for frothing chocolate
Cittern	Citron: a citrus fruit
Corinth	Currants, so named because they came from Corinth
Eringo root	Root of sea holly, candied and prized as an aphrodisiac
Froggs	Smaller form of Landiron
Gibbets	Chimney crane, from which to hang pots over the fire
Grains, Greets or Grits	Coarse oatmeal
Jamaica pepper	Allspice
Land iron	Support for burning wood
Landsettle	Long settle or seat
Lawn sieve	Sieve made from fine linen
Lazy back	Kettle tilter
Malligotoons	A variety of peach, sometimes described as grafted onto a quince
Manchet	The best sort of white bread
Marchpane	A early form of marzipan, usually shaped and eaten by itself
Maw	Stomach bag
Mazarene	A dish upturned over a hearth stone over which hot coals would be heaped to provide an oven.
Mold	Shaped cutter or mould for biscuits
Moutaph	Not known
Mung	From mong, a mixture of grains
Musk	Secreted from the glands of male musk deer, a flavouring
Pastery	Pastry: room where pastry and cakes were prepared
Pig plates	Iron plate used to hold back the heat of the fire
Piggins or lading piggins	Small half barrel with one stave left long to form a handle, used as a ladle
Rundlett	A barrel measuring 18 gallons
Salamandar	Circular iron plate which is heated and placed over a dish to brown it.
Shagreen	Untanned leather usually coloured green
Smoke jack	Device using the rising air from the chimney to turn a spit.
Soo (Sough)	A brewing tub
Sprittle	Probably spirtle or spurtle, either a stick for stirring porridge or a device for turning oatcakes.
Verjuice	Juice of crab apples, fermented
Walm	A boiling up
Warden	Winter cooking pear
Wheel chair	Chair with a wheel back

7. Index to recipes by title

Recipes in **bold** have a modern version.

Plaister for worms in children	60
Preserve Pippin, Pear or warden dry	**53**
Pippin Pudding	**32**
To pott Beef Veal Venison or Hare	22
Puff cakes	48
Quaking pudding	36
Queen cakes	**45**
Quince Marmaylett	**52**
Raisin wine (untitled)	57
Reason wine	59
Raisin wine Mrs Wright	59
Rhumatism	62
Rice pudding	**34**
Sack Posset	**55,56**
Savery Baked Meat	**18**
Scotch collops	**19**
Shrewsbury cakes	**41**
Sillibub	**34**
6 hours pudding	**29**
Small cakes	**44**
Soar throat	60
Infallible cure for a sore throat	63
Soup called Pottage Mager without flesh	22
Sprain	61
Stewed Hare	**20**
Strain in the back sinews of a Horse	61
To stew apples to colour ym	**30**
Sugar cakes	**41**
Syrrup of Buckthorne	62
Tansy pudding	36
Toothach	61
Walnut Catchup	53
White Bread Pudding	**31**
Wiggs	**40**

15. Index to recipes compiled by Thomas Gell (NA DD/E/59/58)

70

1 To preserve Malligotoons.

Take malligotoons & boyle y^m tender in fair wat[er]
& let y^m stand still till they be cold then pare y^m
& pick y^m with a knife to ye stone then put y^m into
as much clarified sugar as will cover them, so let
y^m boyl leisurely 3 or 4 hours you need not fear
breaking y^m for they will boyl like a piece of b[utter?]
when they be boyled tender take y^m up & boyl y^e
syrrup a little by it self, then betwixt hot & cold
you may put y^m up, & keep y^m all ye year.

2 To make cheese puffs.

Take of ye curds of 6 quarts of milk drain it wel[l]
foom ye whey & beat it in a stone Mortar with a b[it]
of butter y^n take ye Yolks of 8 eggs & one white
well beaten, & put it into ye morter wth half a
Pint of very thick cream & one Nutmeg grated
with half a pound of grated & sifted bread wth
sugar & salt mix y^m together to your tast, then make
y^m up with flower ye bigness of a halfpenny loaf &
bake y^m on tinn plates well buttered y^s quantity wil[l]
make nine & half an hour will bake y^m, & when
you have drawn y^m put them into your dish &
powr over y^m some melted butter sack & sugar mixt
a good deal of ye same: if you have any little
tart tinns butter y^m & bake y^s quantity in y^m wthout
any flowr, when they are enough turn y^m out into
ye dish & serve y^m up as you do ye other.

3 To make a Carrot Pudding.

Take two or 3 Carrots grater y^m & two penny whi[te]
loaves gratred & half a pound of fine sugar fin[e]
beaten then take half a pound of butter m[elt?]

To Make a good Cake Lady Gower

Take 12 pound of the finest Flower dry it very well, then
take sixteen pound of Corinth clean washed and Picked they
must be washed in several Waters, the last water must be as
warm as you can bear your hand in it, then drain them and
dry them in a sheet, or two, when so done set them by the fire
to dry, then take a pound and halfe of good powdered Sugar
a Quarter of an ounce of Cloves & Mace a handfull of Salt
two pound and halfe of Raisins of the Sun, Stoned and cut
in Quarters, and dry them, then part your Flower, put one halfe
in ye tub you design to make it in, then strew your Cloves Mace
& Salt into your Flower, then take 3 pints of Cream 6 pound
of butter, and your pound & halfe of Sugar which you
dry'd, and almost a pint of Damask halfe brandy sack best Rose water, set these on ye fire and
make them hot till ye butter be melted but let it not boyl,
take ye yolks of 36 Eggs and halfe ye whites, very well
beaten, then put to them 3 pints of ye best ale yeast, beat
the yeast & Eggs very well together, then strain them into your Flower, as also your Cream
and butter and Rose water and Sugar mix all well together
till all ye Lumps are broken, then take ye rest of your Flower
and strew it all over, and cover it with a Linnen Cloth, and
a Blankett four times doubled, set it before ye fire till
the Flower begins to Crack on ye top, then take it and work
it well together and put in your Raisins & Currans and mix
all well together for a Quarter of an hour, put in two
pound of Almonds beat & Shred, and set it to ye fire to rise
again till your Oven is ready, then make ready your hoop
& cut papers fit for your hoop butter them & stick them
close to your hoop on ye inside with past, when your
oven is ready put your Cake into your hoop, and set into
the Oven, if it colour too much lay a sheet of paper on
the top, so let it stand at least 3 hours before you Ice it
then take a pound & halfe of double refined Sugar beat and
searched mix it with a little Rose water & ye white of an
Egg beaten to a froth, Let not your Icing be too thick
when you put it on your Cake set it in ye Oven to dry
add 3 pound of Orange Lemmon pill & Cittern